# LINCOLNSHIRE (
## BESIDE TH
### 1920's to

by

Stanley Naylor

*Dedicated to my parents, Fred and Emma Naylor*

Photographs:
Top:     Boston 'Stump', by kind permission of Guardian Press (Boston) Ltd.
Middle: Fred Naylor, author's father
Bottom: Jack Hall, grandfather to author's wife, Vera

# LINCOLNSHIRE COUNTRY LIFE
## BESIDE THE WASH
## 1920's to 1939

Written, compiled and first published in Great Britain
in the year 2000 by Stanley Naylor.

Copyright © Stanley Naylor 2000.

British Library Cataloguing in Publication Data.

ISBN  0-9527846-3-7

Printed by:
Guardian Press (Boston) Ltd.
Nelson Way
Boston
Lincolnshire, PE21 8TS
United Kingdom

# CONTENTS

# ACKNOWLEDGEMENTS

My first sincere thanks are to the Reverend Thomas of St. Marks Church, Dukinfield, Manchester, to whom I am indebted for inspiring me to write the book in the first place. It occurred almost four years ago during a conversation with him when I was relating the history of where my brother-in-law, Norman Hall was born, who's funeral we were attending. The Reverend Thomas remarked that such information needed to be recorded for posterity, hence the reason for writing this book.

Where does one start writing such a book? It was decided to confine the contents to the late 1920's through to 1939 as near as possible that covers the period when I was conversant with the farming industry. Nothing was found in libraries relating to the district of Kirton Skeldyke, nothing either on Kirton Marsh except it is part of the Wash Estuary.

I am indebted therefore to the following people for their contributions. My thanks to two poetic friends, the late John Walsh for his poem, 'FIRST OF SEASONS', believed to be the last he wrote. John also encouraged me to write some of the poems included in this book, but I'm sure Tennyson can rest peacefully! To Victor Cavendish for his superb poem 'TRUE BLUE YELLOWBELLY', that truly belongs to the folk who live in the Fens, Skeldyke in particular. But it is an unknown author who wrote the song 'THE LINCOLNSHIRE POACHER', which could be attributed to local persons!

Many of the photographs are from the family album and a number I have taken over the past two years. My thanks, however, to the following people who have kindly loaned me some very historic pictures. Ivy and Ray Dixon for some of the farming scenes, Ray, incidentally, was a neighbour living in the 'Tin Huts' in the 1930's. To my sister Margaret for the 1920's photograph of the horse and cart fitted with raves that is typical of the carts used for harvesting. To Tom Richardson for the excellent photo of 'Perseverance' with the wooden wheels pulled by two horses. Mr. & Mrs. Horace Smith provided me with local steam threshing scenes including the steam threshing engine. To Messrs. Elsey's, Gosberton, for the picture of two 29 seated coaches similar to those used by the Cropley's in the 1930's. To Robert H. Crawford for the Gyro Tiller and Portable Steam Engine illustrations and information.

Norman Loveday for the Fleet Corner and Boat and Gun flood scenes and Father Ashwell demonstrating the use of a scythe. Jack Hall, Seadyke, for a flood photo and 1922 harvest scene. Sid Kime and F. Oliver, the latter from Dorset, for the three horses binding corn. To the Lillian Ream Trust for the harvest scenes and Blacksmith's Forge, and to Mrs. Bratley for the 1947 snow scene.

The following kindly allowed me to take photographs of their machinery, for which I am most grateful. Fred Coupland and Museum of Lincolnshire Life, Steam Cultivating Engines. R. J. Heugh & Son, Steam-Roller. Julian Proctor, a fine display of implements similar to ones I used in the 1930's. Allied Forces Military Museum for the Search Light and Northcote Heavy Horse Centre for the Trap.

Many thanks to Ena Hemington for the Tit-Bits, and Chris Williams for many hours assisting with the proof reading. Thank you to the ladies in both the Kirton and Boston Libraries for being so patient and helpful. I also wish to express my appreciation to the Guardian Press, Boston Standard Newspaper and Boston Reference Library for permission to produce the Skeldyke Village News and Advertisements from the 1930's. The staff at the Guardian Press (Boston) Ltd., have also been brilliant in the help given in producing this book. A special thanks also to Gerald and Richard Barton for helping me to operate this modern contraption, the computer.

I wish to express my thanks and appreciation to my good friends Anne and Boyd Brackenridge and son, Alasdair, in collating all my bits and pieces which is how this book has been compiled. Although there has been a number of setbacks and rejections over the past four years, everyone closely associated with the writing of the book have encouraged me to keep moving forward. As also has my son Keith and his school teacher wife, Chris, in Australia. I also appreciate the bits and pieces I have gleaned from my two brothers, Bill and Cliff, and they all assure me the book has historical value. I hope they are right and that it proves to be a success.

Should I have inadvertently missed thanking anyone for any help given, then my sincere apologies.

*Stanley Naylor, September 2000*

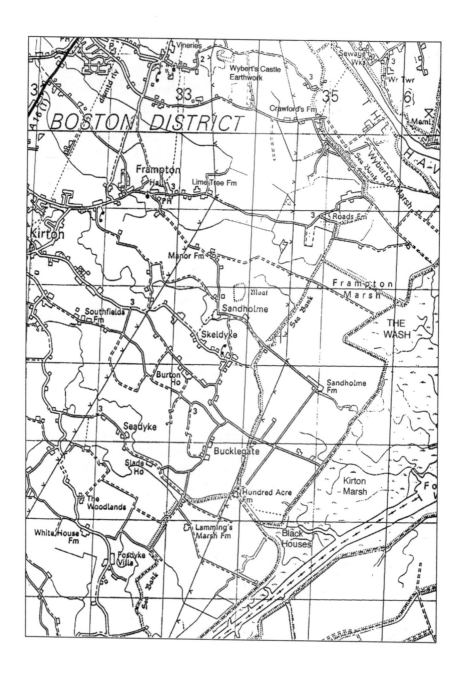

# FIRST OF SEASONS

Not now the scattered crimson fire of poppies,
    Strewn scarlet bright -
Across drowsy English summer fields.
    Too soon yet by far;  for darting swallows,
That swoop and curve and balk high
    On a cerulean blue so warm and clear.
Early yet alas;  to watch surging billows
    Move slowly through golden fields of fast ripening corn.


But come!  Walk with me awhile,
    To see this first of seasons.
This promise of summer on the dawning year.
    Where quiet seas of nodding golden daffodils
Gild brightening verdant meadows with yellow glory.
    Now misty dustings of slender bluebells haze,
Quiet woodlands with purple beauty.
    Where but the silver ringing tones of singing
Birds break the sighing windblown peace.
    In springtime.

© *John R. Walsh, Spring 1996*

# A DESCRIPTION OF
# MY LINCOLNSHIRE COUNTRYSIDE - 1930's

This is something not easily put into words. My early life was spent in a small community engrossed in living a simple life. There was passion, joy, love, happiness, laughter, courage and loyalty. The community spirit was everywhere, it had humour, honour, trust and compassion.

It could be seen in the children trudging to and from school, in their learning, playing and love of life.

It could be seen in the parents as they cycled to and from mundane work on the farms, earning a meagre living, but rich in family love.

It could be seen in the homes sitting by a blazing fire in the twilight of an evening.

It was on a summer's day when the community assembled at a garden fete, at a whist drive on a winter's night and at a concert in the local hall.

When a child was born it was an addition to the community family. A wedding was a joyous occasion for everyone even though they may not attend the event. A death was a severe loss to this close knit community with everyone grieving and offering their condolence to the bereaved family.

It all added up to a peaceful countryside with a tranquillity that was unique.

Where the trees and the flowers were a joy to behold, where the birds and the bees made their home and animals were part of life. Where the rain and the wind were all part of every day living even when the former caused floods and the latter devastated the crops. Where the sun shone on this wonderful countryside and the 'Man in the Moon' was almost real. Where the frost and the snow created a traditional Christmas and Santa Claus was said to come down the chimney!

Was this countryside a religion? I don't know. However, I do know it was real in the 1920's and 30's and a joyful part of my life.

*Stanley Naylor, 2000*

# COUNTRYSIDE CHILDHOOD

Fields and homesteads under a blue sky,
    Birds on the wing, the nightingale sings.
The sun's first rays kissing the heads of corn,
    With a touch of gold in the early dawn.

The wagoner rises to greet the new day,
    Horses are groomed, watered and fed,
Harnessed to the wagon, a touch of the reigns,
    The horses move off, nothing need be said.

Summer arrives producing rich blazing colours,
    Gardens full of flowers with decorative borders,
Trees galore laden with delicious fruit,
    The countryside a picture, everything so beaut!

Dandelions, daisies, buttercups adorn the roadside,
    Pheasants and partridges preening with pride.
Hedges a variety of colour all year round,
    Mother nature providing a paradise on the ground.

Golden corn waving in the breeze,
    We thank you Lord for food grown with ease.
For land so rich, the sun and rain,
    The fruits of labour producing the grain.

The countryside is a magical place,
    Full of freedom and effortless grace.
Where creativity blossoms through the day and night,
    And man goes forth unafraid, as is his right.

© *Stanley Naylor*

# KIRTON SKELDYKE

'Lincolnshire Country Life Beside the Wash' features Kirton Skeldyke (*see map*) in the era of my school days and youth up to the outbreak of war in September 1939.

Skeldyke was, and still is, a hamlet some six miles from Boston. The top end that I refer to as 'Leicester Square', maybe known to some locals as 'Kirton Corner' and 'Hyde Park Corner'. However, it is one mile from the village of Kirton and east of the new A16 road built on the old London North Eastern Railway (LNER) line. Skeldyke Road forks to the left at 'Leicester Square', as per the hand drawn map, and Skeldyke is 2.1 miles in circumference returning to the 'Square'.

Following Skeldyke Road from the 'Square', the first house on the right is Blossom Hall, it was built in 1617 constructed of red brick with a Welsh slate roof. The notable features are the stack of four chimneys that are moulded octagonal twisted brick shafts.

Just along the road in the 1930's was an old chapel built in the 1800's and extended prior to the turn of the century, but still proved to be too small in the early 1900's and a new chapel was built further down the road. The old chapel survived through the two wars ending its days being used for farm storage and some years later was demolished.

Not far from the old chapel was the shell of a 'mud and stud' house believed to have been owned by the Burton family who lived in the brick house that is still occupied today. It is not known when this 'mud and stud' house was built, but it could easily date back to the 1700's. According to my father, it is believed his father occupied this old house at some time, but there are no records to verify the period. One incident that is vivid in my mind, was part of the corrugated roof being ripped off this old house in a gale force wind in 1937/38 and deposited on the ploughing in the field on the opposite side of the road. Father and myself were ploughing in the field each with a team of two horses and had passed the house only minutes before the incident.

Over on the left of the Skeldyke Road is the Mission Church Hall that has been closed for a number of years, it has recently been converted for residential use. My mother would walk from the 'Tin Huts' every

One incident happened on the Marsh Farm about 1936/37 during a harvest tea break when the horses were tied to a tumbrel munching luscious green clover. Now the horses were still attached to the carts fully harnessed. This meant the bridle was still fitted to the head of the horse with the steel bit in its mouth. Now I could never understand how a horse was able to chew clover with that steel bit in its mouth, but they did without too much trouble. On this occasion we were sitting beside a stook drinking cups of steaming tea and relaxing in beautiful sunshine under a deep blue sky. When suddenly one of the horses turned its head round to get rid of an offending fly and caught a rein in a hook on the shaft of the cart to which it was attached. Consequently the horse was unable to straighten its head and panicked, setting off in reverse gear in a half circle ending up in a dyke. Luckily, and I say luckily, both horse and cart was extricated from the dyke without any damage. The horse was a bit shaken, but soon settled down when it got back to munching clover.

As already mentioned, the time now is in the 1930's when father was still wagoner but only had a stable of five horses, this was the result of the farm changing ownership. No matter how big the stable of horses the hours remained the same. The total in the winter was at least seventy-five hours, this would be increased by ten hours in the harvest season.

A lot of work was involved during the hours in the morning and afternoon in the stable. Father had a system of feeding that didn't need a watch, it depended on how long it took the horses to eat each feed. The main feed consisted of oats, the straw being cut in small pieces mixed with corn and known simply as chaff. When I first left school and joined father in the stable in an afternoon, the corn was cut with a hand cutter. This was extremely hard work, much more harder if the two knives were not kept sharp. I am pleased to say this operation did not last very long and a petrol engine was installed in the chaff house to drive a bigger chaff cutter. Whereas the hand cutter had to be used most days, the mechanical cutter would produce a week's supply in about an hour. The chaff then had to be shaken on a small wire mesh riddle to take out all the long straws.

Father's method of feeding was to put three or four bowls of chaff in a straw based sieve and shake it vigorously to take out as much dust as possible that would filter through the straw mesh.

When available, although not authorised by the farmer, two or three sacks of corn would find their way into the chaff house unseen, well that was the theory!  The corn would be well soaked in water over a period of twenty-four hours and a small portion would be added to the sieve. He would then scoop up a bowl of water from an iron trough.  Now this was not just plain clear water.  Oh no!  I never did know the full recipe, but I do know that a slab of linseed cake would be soaking in the bottom, with a tinge of powdered Mandrake he had dug from a hedge bottom, after watching it mature through the summer.  Then there was a measure of copper sulphate, known as blue vitriol, and there were other ingredients added as required.  I know those five horses were always full of energy and often difficult to manage.

Having filled the sieve and bowl, the contents were conveyed to a steel bottom manger where they were thoroughly mixed and divided between two horses.  This meant three journeys to satisfy the needs of the five horses.  As I have said no watch was needed to time the feeds, because as soon as the manger was clean, the horses started looking round for the next one and so the chains started rattling and also the rhythm of the munching stopped.

In between the feeds there was a lot of work that had to be completed. Chaff cutting has already been mentioned, then there was grooming the horses, checking and cleaning harness, greasing cart and wagon wheels, then in the winter, straw was required to bed the covered crew-yard. Last, but by no means least, the stable floor had to be cleaned, known as 'mucking out'.  But why did I get the job so often?

Farm workers, perhaps unknowingly, were put into categories.  The lowest being the labourer who lived in a tied house and was known as a plod, even though he was generally a skilled worker.  Garthmen were one step up the ladder that tended cattle, usually during the winter when cattle was in the farm yard, known as a crew-yard.  I suspect the name Garthman is derived from the word Garth that means yard or paddock, and it always sounded to be pronounced like Gathm'n.

A wagoner was respected and just one step away from being a foreman, both living in tied cottages, as did the garthman.  Besides being skilled in feeding horses, a wagoner had to know how to set and adjust all kinds of implements including ploughs, skerries, potato ridger and hiller, drills, binder, reaper and various other implements, wrong settings could easily destroy a crop. It was usually the wagoner who stacked the corn, which I always thought was a precarious job walking on slippery sheaves close to the edge of a stack.

Perhaps I am biased, but I realised working with father that he was highly skilled in his profession and could so easily have taken the job of foreman on any farm. However, his love of horses was paramount and Skeldyke was his home. To obtain a foreman's job would have meant moving to another district. Then in August 1947 he was taken ill with infantile paralysis/Poliomyelitis and was never to work again, remaining an invalid until 1979 when he died at the age of eighty-four years.

Foremen, wagoners and garthmen were assured of regular work come rain or shine, whereas the labourers like myself had often to go home losing pay in the process. There were wet day jobs such as white washing inside buildings, and one job in particular would have health authorities banning it today. Before drilling corn, it was dressed with a bluish/green powder, not sure for what reason, although I was informed it was to deter birds from eating the grain before it started growing. It was, however, the method of mixing powder and corn that caused problems. One way was to put the corn on a clean concrete floor and spread the powder on top, then turn the corn over with a shovel, similar to mixing cement. This caused clouds of dust from the powder and was not very pleasant regarding breathing. Then an old milk churn was brought into use for the mixing of the two ingredients. I'm not sure this method was any improvement, it was certainly better for the mixing process, but when the lid was removed and the dressed corn was tipped back into the hessian sacks, there was still clouds of dust that caused breathing problems.

Should the cause of having to stop work be just a passing storm, then we would adjoin to a nearby shed, preferably with a dirt floor, a crew-yard or wagon hovel was ideal. 'Pitch and Toss' was the game we played, totally illegal and it certainly cost me money I could ill afford as a young teenager. A losing streak causes one to learn quickly and I soon began to recoup losses.

The dictionary tells us that Lady Day, one of the quarter days in England and Wales, is the 25th March. However, before World War II, locally the 6th April was recognised as 'Lady Day', and perhaps that tradition prevails today. On the 6th of April farm workers changed their jobs, moving from one farm to another. Should the 6th fall on a Saturday, then this was considered not a good day to move. As the saying goes; 'Saturday Flit-Not-Long-To-Sit'. To avoid the Saturday Flit, some workers moved on the Friday, or even waited until the Monday.

The reason for moving was varied. Some workers liked to change jobs every year for perhaps no valid reason at all, but this caused havoc with families, no stable relationships with neighbours, certainly no stable education for the children. Other reasons included the prospect of earning more money, better working conditions, a better house, nearer a shop and school, there were no school buses in the 1920's. Or perhaps it was to be nearer a pub, as this drew some men like a magnet with no thought of the family. Then there could have been a dispute with the foreman or boss, or they didn't fit in the community anyway. I have to say that working conditions in the Skeldyke were very good and attracted a good class of worker, many of them staying on the same farm for years.

It was in the late 1920's that the Ashwell family arrived in Bucklegate to a house just behind the Sycamore Farm close to the border of Skeldyke. The house was typical of those in the area, no gas, electricity, piped water or telephone, with the privy down the garden path. Access was down a stone lane with grass growing down the centre in many places. My family was their neighbours from 1940 to 1948 in the same lane but the houses were some two hundred and fifty to three hundred yards apart.

Mr. William Henry Ashwell was respected and affectionately known by our elders as 'Father' Ashwell, as children he was always addressed as Mr. Ashwell. In fact that was how I always addressed him up to the age of twenty-seven when I moved into the village of Kirton in 1949 and lost touch with this grand old man.

One of the first encounters with Mr. Ashwell as children was getting a warm welcome knocking on his door on Guy Fawkes night and being greeted with 'You're Fred Naylor's kids'. The house was also passed on our way to and from our grandparents in 'Field House'. When grandmother offered us a chicken I had to carry it live for almost a half-mile to the Ashwell abode to be killed either by Mr. Ashwell or his son, Charles. Then when my father killed a pig, not literally, Charlie Bishop and Tom Cowham carried out that operation, Mr. Ashwell with his son Charles would arrive in the evening to cut-up the carcass to be placed in a tub ready for salting. Both the tripod on which the pig had been hung all day and the cratch it laid on at night were borrowed from Mr. Ashwell.

Mr. Ashwell never attended a school, he could neither read nor write but had a good head for figures that enabled him to be a farm foreman for many years prior to moving to Bucklegate. He never rode a bike or ever attended a cinema. He was one of a large family and knew poverty, starting work at the age of seven for 4d per day (less than 2p in today's currency). Twelve hour days were normal and often much longer, subsequently he worked hard all his life and did not retire until he was around eighty years of age. After retirement he still remained active in a very large garden, see photo of him demonstrating the art of using a scythe.

Mr. and Mrs. Ashwell raised a family of four boys and four girls. Mrs. Ashwell died eleven years prior to Mr. Ashwell who died at the age of ninety-three on the 22nd January, 1957.

When a family moved they usually had no means of transport, furniture removal vans were few and far between, a farm worker would not be able to afford the cost if one was available. The farmer who had hired him would therefore provide free transport and it was a job usually undertook by the wagoner.

Every wagoner, my father included, loved nothing better *(unless it was a pint of beer)* than to parade a team of horses into another district. Horses would be well groomed, harness cleaned, brasses polished and caddis *(coloured ribbon)* plaited in the mains and tails. Two horses would easily haul a wagon for this type of job, but a team of three horses was more impressive, that is two walking side by side in front of one in the shafts of the wagon. There was friendly rivalry between every wagoner, they all took pride in their teams of horses, nothing was left to chance, they each wanted top marks when it was discussed in the pubs at night, especially when it was in another district.

There was another valid reason why my father enjoyed the opportunity to work on the roads. Mother's eldest brother, George, drove a brewer's dray delivering beer to local pubs, so there was a good chance they would meet somewhere on the journey. George would stop and they would crack open a bottle or two of beer and put the world to rights! Same ritual applied if George spotted father working in a field adjacent to the road.

The 'Tin Huts' *(see photo)* was my home for almost eighteen years and I was the eldest of a family of three boys and two girls. All five were born in this abode, mother being attended by the doctor and district nurse. There was no question of going to hospital for a birth for anyone, unless something was seriously wrong, as there was no National Health in those days. Even my son, Keith, was born at home in October 1953 without any problems.

The type of house we lived in was a product of the First World War and is believed to have housed troops, where is not known. Having said that, and from my memory, this double tenement bungalow was in pristine condition and could have been brand new surplus to requirements. We lived in the end as seen in the photo, this proved to be handy when attending school, as we only had to cross the road. There was no more of this construction in the Skeldyke, but there were another pair of similar bungalows on Wash Road, Kirton.

It was thought the type of construction of the 'Tin Huts' was the forerunner to the 'Nissen Hut' widely used in the Second World War as accommodation for serving personnel, but this is not so. Having read 'Nissen of the Huts' by Fred McCoosh and lived in them in the Shetland Isles and the UK during the war, I can safely say there is no comparison. The Nissen Hut was constructed of two layers of corrugated iron sheets, the inside layer being horizontal and the outside layer being semi-circular. The walls and roof were therefore semi-circular in shape. Both ends were of wooden construction, one end having two windows and the other end having two windows and a door in the centre. A storm porch was erected outside the entrance as some protection from the severe elements, gale force winds and torrential rain was something to endure in the winter months in the Shetlands. It was said this type of Nissen Hut kept the heat in during the winter and was cool in a hot summer. I'm not so sure about the summer, but in the Shetland Isles during the winter of 1943/44 in an endeavour to keep warm, we had to cover ourselves with six blankets when in bed plus a leather jerkin over our feet. The free-standing iron stove had to be kept burning throughout the night. It was an unwritten rule in the hut that anyone wakening during the night, for whatever reason, had to ensure the fire was well stoked up. Anyone found breaking this rule would cost him a fortune buying beer in the NAAFI for the rest of the residents.

I digress from the story of Skeldyke, but I thought the comparison of the two types of hut were relevant.

The design of the 'Tin Huts' was a single story straight-sided building with an apex roof. The outside walls and roof was constructed with sheets of corrugated iron. Inside there were three bedrooms, each being adequately furnished, including a chamber pot. The latter was essential as the privy was outside some twenty-five/thirty yards down the garden path and not the sort of place to visit during the night. It was a small draughty uncomfortable building with wooden walls and door, with a corrugated iron roof that sounded terrible during an hailstorm. There was a wooden bench type seat and a vault that was emptied once a year, depending on the size of the family! It was ideal for catching up on the news, because toilet papers were torn from sheets of newspapers, proving, of course, that old newspapers were not just used for wrapping up fish and chips.

Returning to the house, the bedrooms opened into the lounge/living/dining room that had a free-standing iron cooking range that was the sole means of heating the whole house. There was a lot of heat from the iron chimney that rose straight through the roof where there was a sheet of asbestos on the ceiling acting as a fire precaution. Sweeping the chimney was a simple task of climbing on the roof and dropping a weighted rope down the pipe with a wisp of straw attached. This was a cheap way of cleaning the chimney and proved very effective.

On one side of this free standing coal fired iron stove was a boiler for heating water, all the cooking being done for a family of seven in the oven on the other side of the fire and on top of the stove.

We had never heard of an en-suite, so there was no bathroom or even a shower. Therefore, Friday was the one night of the week when a large tin bath was placed before the fire with the boys and girls following each other. The water would not be changed because it was a scarce commodity in the 1920's, piped water came later in the 30's. Neither was there any electricity or gas, houses were illuminated with paraffin lamps and candles.

Two more doors opened into the central room in the "Huts", one was into the pantry where there was a charcoal filter that purified the drinking water *(see W. Armes & Co advertisement for an illustration of a water filter)*. Our drinking water came from the cistern sunk in the school playground just over the road. Water caught from the house roof was stored in a square tank stood on bricks at the rear of the building and was used for bathing and washing clothes.

The other door that was next to the pantry opened into a lean-to building that served both as a wash house and coal storage. Coal was purchased at a maximum of two ton, this being the amount that filled a quarter of the space in the lean-to. In the first few years in the opposite corner of that half of the building, was a free standing copper, this was replaced later with a built-in copper that proved more efficient and was used extensively on washdays.

Monday was the traditional day for washing clothes, every house seemed to compete for first place with clothes billowing on a line stretched between two posts beside the garden path. Mother would rise by 6.00 am to have breakfast and a packed lunch prepared for father arriving at 6.15 am. The copper would be filled with water carried from the static tank in a bucket. A fire was then prepared underneath the copper with paper and sticks and eventually fuelled with coal. While the water was being heated, we would be roused from our beds and prepared for school.

The cycle of washing started with sorting the clothes, whites from colours, then hot water being transferred from the copper to a dolly tub in which the first wash would be placed. Then came the back-breaking job of using a dolly peg to turn the clothes in the water. When this cycle was completed the clothes would be transferred to the copper to be boiled for a period of time not known. When the boiling process was completed, the clothes would be passed through a mangle, or wringer. Which ever name the machine was known, the process was very effective, the two rollers squeezing out most of the water, then the clothes would be hung on the garden line.

This washing cycle would continue until all the clothes were hanging on the line, the time taken would easily be four or five hours. Mother would then get down on hands and knees and physically scrub the concrete floor of the wash house. As the clothes dried they were retrieved from the line and returned to the house where a flat iron heated on the fire ironed them. *(See photo of flat irons).*

During the ironing process, mother would be preparing a meal for father arriving at 4.00 pm, the remainder of the ironing being completed during the evening, with mother retiring to bed around 10.30 pm.

**A *survey* published in 1999 stated that the laundry in a modern house was completed in twenty-five minutes. I am not sure if that is correct, but certainly the chore is completed in a lot less time and with a lot less effort than in my mother's day. But what does everybody do with the time saved?**

Floors in the 'Huts' were covered with linoleum, walls were papered and ceilings distempered, as it was called, or white washed. A traditional 'snip' rug, often referred to as a 'peg' rug, was made from old clothes cut into small pieces and pegged to a piece of hessian. This formed a very hard-wearing rug that took pride of place in front of the fire.

A by-product of the coal fire was ash stored in a corner of the garden referred to as a cinder heap. During bad weather in the winter, and often during heavy rain in the summer, the cinders would be spread on the paths around the house up to the road, this formed good and cheap solid paths.

As previously mentioned, the privy was down the garden path with a vault that had to be emptied every year. This was the cause of some people starting to smoke, so I was told, and I was sorely tempted. But I was spared this habit with father blowing clouds of smoke from his pipe that helped to fumigate the air. The contents of the vault were dug in the garden that produced bumper crops of potatoes and brussel sprouts. Like the ash from the fire, nothing was wasted.

My paternal grandparents were both married twice and were a unique couple. Joseph was born in Frampton in 1854 and moved to Skeldyke at a very early age where he lived most of his life. He was a typical farm worker, 'salt of the earth', certainly a Fenman and a Yellowbelly, living in rural Lincolnshire beside the Wash. Joseph was employed by four generations of the Tunnard family, his starting wage was 6d (2½p) per week and is understood to have never earned more than twelve shillings (60p) per week. His second wife, Alice, was also born in 1854.

Joseph's first wife was Eliza Johnson who died at an early age leaving him with nine children. Alice Johnson married David Suley and they lived in Horncastle, but David also died at an early age leaving his wife with six children.

When Joseph married Alice, he therefore married two sisters, Eliza and Alice Johnson. The second marriage for both of them started with the daunting task of having a ready made family of fifteen children. This seemed not enough because they produced three more to make the total eighteen. Louie born in 1891 married Tom Burton and lived at Peterborough. Earnest born in 1893 and emigrated to Canada in 1910 never to see his parents again. The third and last was Fred, my father, born in 1895. These eighteen children eventually produced fifty-two grandchildren.

Two grass fields had to be crossed to reach the tied cottage in which Joseph and Alice lived, hence it being named 'Field House'.

Typical of this type of house, there were no mod cons, therefore no bathroom, just four large bedrooms with the essential chamber pot, the privy being down the garden path. Downstairs there was a front room, often referred to as a parlour. There were no such things as fridges and freezers, so a cold pantry in 'Field House' was useful in the summer. There was a square wooden frame covered with very fine mesh supported on four legs, where food such as meat was stored to keep it away from flies. There was also the charcoal filter that purified the water drawn from a cistern sunk in the ground just outside the one and only door in the house. The cistern being filled with water caught from the roof of the house.

The main living room had the traditional black coal fire iron grate built in the wall with a boiler on one side and oven on the opposite side. This was where all the cooking was done, except perhaps in the heat of the summer when there was no coal fire, cooking would be done on a Valour three burner paraffin stove. There was no electricity, gas, wireless or telephone. Their sole means of transport was on 'shanks's pony'. Grandma walked a mile each way twice a week to collect fresh milk from a farm and two miles each way to Kirton once a fortnight to collect pensions and essential shopping. The Co-Op (Co-Operative Society) van called every Saturday with groceries and paraffin, and coal was purchased in bulk.

Contact with the outside world was limited, there was a fair amount of post from such a large family causing the postman to call two or three times every week. For many years this was Mr. Pettit who always received a cup of tea with biscuits, a much-needed refreshment after cycling down a rough lane and over the two grass fields.

Often during the summer months, 'Field House' would be a hive of activity, full of love and laughter from some of the huge family of relatives enjoying a few days holiday. Many of them forfeiting the mod cons they were used to at home to enjoy the fresh air, sunshine and pleasant walks around the fields and lanes, far removed from the hustle and bustle of city life, even in those days in the 1920's and early 30's.

Ralph, a late cousin and a self-employed accountant, lived in Leicester. He mentions in his autobiography that there was more protocol in this house of a farm labourer than any other house he had visited. For example, no one was permitted to sit in either grandma's or grandfather's chairs without permission. Likewise we were not permitted in the parlour, only on special occasions such as Christmas. Children were seen and not heard woe-be-tide any child breaking this rule, as one brother and sister can vouch for the consequences. Ralph also mentions the occupants of 'Field House' produced their own vegetables, they always had twenty or more chickens, and in his early years grandfather fed and killed a pig every year. So visitors were always greeted with eggs and bacon for breakfast, with fresh mushrooms picked from the dewy grass fields. Ralph also mentions Grandfather taking a piglet to Boston market and selling it for 6d. (2½p) and getting drunk on the proceeds on the way home. Grandfather loved a glass or two of good ale, but this incident wouldn't please grandmother.

Grandmother always wore a piece of lace up to her neck when dressed for visitors and grandfather wore a bow tie, as seen in a photograph later in the book. Grandfather also taught me how to sew a button on a shirt and darn socks that proved very useful in later life during my service career. They certainly set a standard of behaviour that I was pleased to adopt and have tried to uphold, that may not have been as successful as I would have hoped.

Grandfather had the philosophy that nothing should be wasted, hence the elder hedge and the privy was a source of invaluable products. The elder hedge down one side of his garden was some thirty-five/forty yards long and produced flowers that were picked to make wine. This was a drink we were denied and I wondered why. Then one Sunday at a family gathering when the wine was flowing freely, I saw the elders getting flushed faces and becoming exceptionally talkative! And grandmother was a staunch Methodist! The entire flower would not be picked for wine, enough would be left to form berries to be gathered later in the year to be made into syrup. Elder berry syrup had the reputation, and perhaps still does, of being good for colds and sore throats, so we were allowed, even encouraged, to drink the syrup. I'm sure the wine would have tasted better!

Elder sticks grow to a height of six or seven feet, about two metres in today's language. In the late autumn they would be cut at the base and tied in bundles. The following year these sticks would be used to support kidney beans to enable them to climb and mature. At the end of the bean season the sticks would be re-bundled.

Grandfather's privy was a brick building with a tiled roof, there was the traditional wooden bench seat with the vault that needed to be emptied every year. He was of the opinion that the content was too strong to go straight on the garden, so it was emptied into a pit and allowed to mellow. To avoid accidents such as some one falling into the pit, the used bundles of bean sticks were placed over the top. The following year the contents of the pit was dug in the garden making excellent manure for the vegetables. I wonder if this would come under the term of organic gardening? The bundles of sticks that came off the top of the pit were chopped into a suitable size and used to light the house fire. This cycle of jobs took place every year, proving that the elder hedge and privy provided valuable products.

I never knew my grandparents to be ill, apart from severe colds which they always doctored themselves. Then old age caught up with grandfather and although he was seriously ill he did not go to hospital, but stayed in 'Field House', where he died in 1936 just one month before his eighty-third birthday. He was given a funeral in farming tradition. A horse and trolley transported the coffin over the two grass fields, down the gravel lane to the Skeldyke Methodist Chapel in Marsh Road.

At thirteen years of age, this was the first funeral I had attended and I have strong memories of the two hymns sung at the service, 'Abide with Me' and 'Rock of Ages Cleft for Me'. The service was a fitting tribute to a fine man and a loving grandfather.

After the service a farm lorry transported the coffin to Kirton Cemetery. Local farmers loaned the horse, trolley and lorry, all part of the community spirit that prevailed in the Skeldyke.

Alice vacated 'Field House' and moved to Peterborough to live with her daughter, Louie. Grandmother had already survived the First World War and lived through the Second World War, dying in 1948 at ninety-four years of age. She was buried beside Joseph in Kirton Cemetery. Perhaps simple living standards and a large family is the recipe for a long life. Who knows?

There were no more than forty houses in the Skeldyke where some 170 inhabitants lived, most of them farm workers. It was a farming community with families of five, six and seven being common place. Of course, there was no television! All the houses were the same as the 'Tin Huts' and 'Field House', no gas, electricity and the privy down the garden path with the wooden seat and vault.

Farming in the 1920's and 30's was hard both for man and horse. In the spring, teams of horses would be cultivating the arable fields preparing them for planting the crops. For example, no less than eleven horses, five men and a youth were required for drilling corn. There would be one man with three horses pulling a spring tined drag. Following the drag would be a man and three horses with a set of three heavy harrows. Two men, a youth and three horses operating the drill, and one man with two horses and a set of three light harrows covering the drilled corn.

Setting potatoes required no less than fourteen people and twelve horses. Two men with six horses cultivating with spring tine drag and heavy harrows. Two horses on a three row ridger preparing the rows in which the tubers would be planted, usually a job undertaken by the wagoner. One man and a horse operated a three-row guano (fertiliser) spreader. Prior to the introduction of this mechanical spreader, the job was performed manually with a hopper strapped to a man's chest. As each forward step was taken a handful of guano was scooped from the hopper and spread on the prepared rows. It was a rhythmic movement that continued until the hopper was empty, the job was hard work and very dirty.

Two men with one horse and trolley transported the boxes of tubers to the field, to be set by a gang consisting of a man to oversee six or eight women. Operating in pairs in a rhythmic movement, one right handed and one left handed pulling a box between them, as each step was taken backwards a tuber would be lifted from the box and planted in the prepared rows. Fortunately I only did this job on one occasion during an Easter school holiday in 1936, which I found back breaking and very hard work. To complete this operation, a man with two horses and a three-row hiller covered the 'tates', the man also collected the empty boxes and stacked them at the end of the rows. In my view the setting of the 'tates' was very demeaning for the women, so it was a great relief for them when a mechanical planter was introduced.

Harvest time provided work for many people, even five or six Irishmen would be hired on a temporary basis, their living conditions in the cake-house being sparse, to say the least. When the corn was almost ripe, one man with a scythe would cut a swathe round the outside of the field. The scythe would be sharpened with a round rub stone carried in a hugger fitted to his belt. The mown corn would be tied in sheaves by twisting strands of the corn to make the tie. The swathe would be wide enough to allow three horses to walk side-by-side pulling a self-binder *(see photo)*. Two men and two teams of three horses would operate the

32

binder working shifts of two hours each. The team of horses resting would be tied to a tumbrel and fed fresh clover, while their driver would be sharpening a set of knives ready for his next shift on the binder. This operation continued through daylight hours, weather permitting, heavy dew often delayed any early start.

The next link in the harvest process was a gang of six or eight men picking-up the sheaves from two rows and standing them eight or ten to a stook. There is a true story of a gang of stookers complaining to the foreman that there were too many thistles in the sheaves. Now thistles can grow as high as the corn and when dry have prickles as sharp as needles badly scratching the arms of the stookers. They were not looking for sympathy but a rise in their piecework rate as compensation, so the reply was not one they wanted. The foreman was not only hard, but also wise in such dealings. Having omitted all the colourful phrases, the gist of the reply was; 'If you had not spent so much time resting at the ends of the field when you were supposed to have been hoeing the weeds in the spring, those thistles would not be causing you problems today'. The foreman smiled as he departed quickly in his truck.

The stooks allowed the corn to dry and when hard the sheaves would be transported from the field to the farmyard to be either threshed or stored in a stack. The threshing process was a high labour intensive job that required at least a dozen people. Two men were required in the field to load the horse drawn carts. Depending on distance, one or two boys, or women, would lead the horses to and from the field. One man teemed the sheaves from the cart placing them on the platform of the threshing drum. The sheaves were picked-up by either a boy or woman, who cut the bands and placed the loose corn in the arms of a man standing in a well feeding the corn into the beaters. One man working at the front of the drum filled, weighed and carried the sacks of corn onto a trolley. The weights varied: twelve stone for oats; sixteen stone for barley; eighteen stone for wheat and the heaviest was nineteen stone for beans. Chaff oozing from the side of the drum kept one man busy carrying it to a shed for storage. The straw was carried up an elevator to be stacked by two or three men, the number being determined by the size of the stack.

Country folk waste nothing that can be put to good use and threshing provided some useful products. The bands, or string as it might be known, were saved from the sheaves and used throughout the year for tying various sacks *(see glossary)*. Wheat chaff was fed to the cattle in the winter. Straw provided clean bedding in the crews for cattle and horses, it was also used for thatching corn stacks, (referred to as thacking) and was also used for covering 'tatie' graves, or clamps.

Cutting clover required two men each with a team of two horses working in rotation the same as cutting corn. Clover was grown to feed horses, any surplus would be dried, baled and sold often to racing stables. Before being baled or even stored in a stack, clover had to be perfectly dry. It can generate tremendous heat causing instantaneous combustion if some of it is still green when tightly compressed. I did witness on one occasion when a stack of clover was opened to feed cattle, the centre was as black as coal and was obvious it had been close to causing a fire that would have destroyed the stack. Certainly a timely reminder that green products need to be absolutely dry before being compressed.

An incident occurred one year while cutting clover involving a 'gentlemen' walking between Boston and Spalding following a public footpath beside the field being harvested near 'Leicester Square'. A cart had been left in the field over night under it had been made a bed of clover that had provided the occupant a free night's accommodation. Although free, it was rather short on en-suite facilities and breakfast.

In the spring when cattle and horses were turned loose in grass fields, there would be a depth of four or five feet of manure in the crews. Hence the job well known in farming as simply 'muck carting'. This entailed three men, each with a four tined fork loading the manure on horse drawn carts. The horses would be lead by boys to a corner of a field where a man would tip the manure for storage during summer. In the autumn the manure would again be loaded on horsedrawn carts and spread on the field to be used as fertiliser.

Potatoes provided an enormous amount of work throughout the year starting in the winter with seed potatoes being taken into the glass house in eight stone sacks. There were several varieties, some once grown on the farm, but the majority would be Scotch seed. Transferring the seed from sacks to boxes was a job for a wet day, or when snow and frost prevented work in the fields. Each sack was emptied evenly into three boxes. Each box measured thirty inches long, eighteen inches wide with three and half-inch sides. The two six inch corner posts at each end of the box had a handle attached. The corner posts had to be strong, as the boxes were stacked fifteen to twenty high, depending on the height of the glass house, or green house, as they were often referred. To reach up to these heights, the boxes were carried on our heads climbing a ladder. To try and make the job as comfortable as possible, a thick ring of wheat straw was woven to fit the crown of the head. A bit like a 'halo' I suppose, although I can assure the reader that a box of potatoes weighing close to three stone sitting on a cushion of straw was still very heavy and very uncomfortable. During the winter months the glass house was heated by a freestanding coke fired stove, this was the place for lunch when those east winds were blowing over the marshes.

Planting potatoes has already been described, the first crop would be harvested early summer. New potatoes have tender skins and would be packed in six stone barrels with green foliage tied on top to try and get the product to market without being damaged and so turning brown. As the skins hardened, then eight stone hessian sacks were used. Most of the late crop would be stored in a grave, or clamp, at the end of the field beside a good tarmac road. A layer of straw would cover the potatoes, then later two layers of soil would be packed on top of the straw by men using spades and brute strength. Hence the reason the top of the grave would only get two thin layers of soil, it's a long way to the top from the bottom of a trench that is being dug to obtain the soil. To compensate for the lack of soil, a layer of dried grass, known as hovers, sounds like huvers, would cap the grave.

When prices were buoyant in the winter, a gang of four men working in unison would open the grave. On arriving at the grave in the morning, the first job was to remove about nine or ten yards of soil and then erect a sheet to give some shelter from the elements. Two men operated two wire mesh riddles, the size being determined by the market. They were placed on stands, one each side of a weighing machine. The third man filled the riddles using a large screen, the fourth weighed and tied the sacks of potatoes. As each ten sacks were filled, so the team moved round one place clockwise, this procedure afforded some exercise in avoiding getting frozen stiff at these riddles.

When horses and trolley arrived, a two man 'icking stick' was used to lift the eight stone sacks of potatoes that had to be carried shoulder high, often over a slippery plank that made the job precarious. Extra padding was rarely used that resulted in a sore shoulder carrying these eight stone sacks.

There was a lot of mischievous devilry amongst the team, daring one another to achieve almost impossible tasks. One of the team was the late Walter Willerton, who was the last landlord of the 'Boat and Gun'. His daughter, Vilma, has recently reminded me of our weight lifting feats that her father talked about many times over a pint of beer with customers. One or two of us could easily stand straight up lifting two four stone weights in each hand. One of the team could put two four stone weights in a scuttle and lift it onto his shoulder, I found that impossible only getting the scuttle up to my chest. The ultimate was being dared to carry three sacks of potatoes over a plank, which I achieved with some difficulty. Mixed with all the banter was camaraderie that I'm certain was a grounding that helped me to mix with strangers on joining the Royal Air Force, and I am proud to add the last bit, the RAF Regiment.

Many jobs on the farm were annual including cleaning out dykes trying to keep the waterways clear so that water drained from the Fens could flow unheeded to the pumps that helped it on its way to the Wash. Hedges needed trimming and the hedge bottoms dug where the plough could not reach, One of the most dawdling jobs was weeding corn that I found boring, there was more movement weeding potatoes, but still not a good job.

Sugar beet created a lot of work. There was the usual cultivation by teams of horses, but more care was needed to create a finer soil than for other crops. One horse easily pulled a four-row drill, again a job for the wagoner leading the horse with a measured stick, with a man following to ensure even distribution of seed. Consequently as the plants grew they were too close together and when high enough were 'chopped out', known as 'gapping', by the men with six or seven inch hoes. A skilled man who concentrated on his work would often leave just a single plant, but mostly the plants were left in multiples. This entailed another back-breaking job for the women, known as singling sugar beat. A man and wife team would earn extra money taking a measured acre to gap and single at a special rate. This favoured the man who could gap the beat leaving as many single plants as possible. There would be another session of weeding by hand with perhaps the horse hoe being used twice, the crop would then be left to mature.

Lifting sugar beet followed the harvest. See the photo of a plough pulled by two horses and operated by one man. Sugar beet grows deep like parsnips, so the plough only loosened the beet. It was then the job of the men to literally pull the beet out of the ground and with one in each hand knock them together to remove as much soil as possible. The beet was laid in straight rows, it then required a sharp knife held in one hand to chop off the leaves, being careful not to cut one's own feet, the other hand picking up the beet and throwing it into heaps. Another back-breaking job done in a rhythmic movement. Horses and carts would collect the heaps and either transport the beet straight to the Railway Station, or store it in a heap near the road to be moved later when required by the factory. Fortunately I only got involved one season in the lifting process, but it was another of those jobs best done at a piecework rate that gave the opportunity to earn some extra cash. It was extremely hard work, then there was the weather to take into consideration, frosty mornings and rainy days made the job even harder.

Winter deep ploughing to a depth of around ten inches required three horses, whereas five or six inches for planting cabbage could be done by two horses. Big boned horses such as Shires and Clydesdales would pull their own weight of around a ton on a wooden wheeled cart on a dry arable field, on a tarmac road the same horse would pull one and quarter ton. A team of three horses would haul a five-ton load on a wagon with well-greased wooden wheels, this was the usual order for potatoes to be loaded on a railway truck.

In 1928, against all odds and criticism, father won a prestigious ploughing match competition. Then a year or two later he won the best horse and cart competition at a local show. I was with him on this occasion and could not understand why we had to go the long way round through Frampton on the way home. We did, of course, stop at the 'Moores Arms', which mother explained was a favourite pub of his when they were courting. No doubt father was proud of his achievement and it was a pub where he would meet rival wagoners. We didn't get past the

'Boat and Gun' either, something I omitted to tell mother, well I was bribed with a bottle of pop and crisps, although father said it was payment for looking after the horse, and me only eight or nine years of age. Father had a canny way with horses, they would do his bidding with quiet words of command. I never knew him raise his voice or actually beat a horse, a sharp flick of the reins always produced the results required. Although I never was cruel to them I often seemed to be in trouble. I was returning one afternoon from Blossom Hall to the Sycamore Farm with Jolly and an empty trolley, congratulating myself I had timed it just right to be at base at 4.00 pm, the end of the working day. Now from the old 'Barn House' to the 'Boat and Gun' corner, although it may not appear so, there was a very shallow slope that was just enough for the trolley to push Jolly into a canter that may have only lasted a couple of hundred yards. I didn't try to restrain him but let him move at his own pace and slow to walking pace in his own time. Unfortunately father saw the incident, even though he was at least a half-mile away. Consequently on arriving in the stable I received another lecture on heavy horses such as Jolly not being allowed to canter, it was not good for their health. Jolly did sweat profusely on this occasion and took some time to cool down. Once again proving father to be correct.

Working with horses after leaving school often meant working with Trimmer. He was a very intelligent, big boned, strong horse with a mind of his own, this meant that very often we were not working in unison. Had I known then what I know now, we might have had a better working relationship. Trying to put on his collar when I was only fourteen/fifteen years of age was a major problem. Trimmer would hold his head high almost out of my reach and did on one occasion plant a foot on top of mine, without putting on too much weight I might add, but it was his way of letting me know he was in charge. Father would be hiding in the chaff house chuckling at my predicament, there was no offer of help, I had to learn the hard way.

Mangolds was a root crop grown to feed cattle in the winter that was stored in a grave in the field until required. The roots then had to be moved from the field to a shed at the Sycamore Farm. Trimmer and I had been allotted this job and the first load of the day had been delivered without incident. As we approached 'Fleet Corner' on the second

38

journey, Trimmer decided he had done enough and actually got the bit between his teeth, turned round and we promptly went back to the farm, without me being able to stop him. It was fortunate that no one witnessed what had happened. After a five-minute respite Trimmer decided we could continue with the job in-hand and nothing further happened, that day anyway.

Cultivating between rows of potatoes was known as skerrying, not a good job because the implement had to be partially carried otherwise it would be impossible for the horse to pull it. This was another job Trimmer and I had been allotted as a team. Being rather clever, or so I thought, I was trying to drive the horse with only one rein, well father had no trouble driving one horse, Trimmer included, or a team of three horses with just the one rein. Now with more experience I would have noticed Trimmer getting agitated, but I blissfully carried on when suddenly Trimmer decided enough was enough and promptly left me stranded in the middle of the field. Galloping almost a quarter of a mile back to the farm, with the implement on its side, broke off all bolt heads, the bolts being the means of setting the depth of the tines on the skerry. The job was eventually resumed with two reins, which I should have used in the first place, it would have saved me not only getting a very sharp tongue from the foreman but there was another lecture from father. This really was a tough apprenticeship, then if that wasn't enough, the following incident occurred.

Father was aware I hated working a skerry, he asked if I thought I could manage Turpin and Farmer, two frisky animals he had been breaking-in, who by this time were mature Welsh horses. It was agreed we would change jobs on the understanding that at no time would the reins leave my hands, I'll leave you to work out the problems that were caused for lunch and toilet requirements, and I was only to ride Turpin to and from the field. The normal procedure for riding a working horse was bareback in a sideways position. With a two-horse team it was the left-hand horse that was ridden, Turpin in this case with Farmer on the right and both horses being driven on the right-hand side of the road. Everything had worked perfectly for four days I could not have wished for them to have behaved any better. There had been good weather during the week and on the fifth day the sun was shining beautifully under a clear blue sky. We left a Marsh field at lowsin-time and negotiated the 'Pullover' and there standing on the left-hand side of the road was a brand new cart loaded with new white potato boxes. Had I read the mood of the horses correctly I would have dismounted and lead them past this distraction. Being clever, I remained seated until Turpin kicked up his heels and threw me off and they ran unattended straight to the stable. I was only slightly bruised but my pride was badly dented and I had to walk the half-mile to the Sycamore Farm. On arrival I found the horses already in their stalls and father waiting to give me yet another lecture, which I suppose I deserved.

Mrs. Bratley gave me this story that was much more serious. About nine o-clock on the 10th September 1891, yes that was the date, Miss. Alice Tunnard, daughter of Mr. Robert Tunnard of Kirton Bucklegate, was taking her two sisters to Kirton School in a pony carriage. At the last house on the left in Nidds Lane stood a rag and bone man's handcart at which the horse took fright. Consequently the carriage was overturned in the dyke, the two girls were thrown clear and unharmed but Miss. Tunnard was trapped underneath and died.

These stories clearly show that when horses are docile they should not be taken for granted, drivers needed to be on their toes at all times ready for the unexpected. In my case it was a matter of learning lessons the really hard way!

I am, believe it or not, very fond of horses, they are highly intelligent and lovely animals, as Trimmer has already proved. Working with them entailed a lot of walking which family and friends know I hate. It may not be generally known, and I have done no measurements, but it is understood that to plough an acre, skerry three and chain harrow twelve acres of potatoes, drill, harrow or horse hoe twelve acres of corn, each job involved walking no less than ten miles. Another mile at least could be added doing all the jobs in the stable morning and night, giving another valid reason for me not wanting to follow in father's footsteps!

During the summer months when the horses were in the grass field, father only had to appear at the gate and they would surround him in seconds. He could almost drive them with words of command, but two taught reins was required to draw a straight rig. First of all two wads, pieces of wood six or seven feet long each with ten or twelve inches of white paper attached at the top would be placed at a measured distance at the far end of the field. Then came the tricky job of keeping the wad at the back in line with the one at the front looking between the two horses pulling the plough. The second furrow would be ploughed away from the first, then both ploughed inwards so forming a rig, or ridge. I wonder why my rig often took the shape of a half moon? Proving the true wagoner was a rare breed of men dedicated to their profession.

A farm horse wore a bridle with blinkers. These were pieces of leather at the side of the eyes to try and keep them looking straight ahead, the object being to avoid them being startled. This didn't always work, as previous stories have proved. A halter would be used to catch a loose horse and to tie it to a tumbrel when a bridle was removed. It was better for the horse eating when the bridle was removed and the bit taken out of its mouth. The bit controls the horse guiding it by means of the reins in the direction it is required to go. The breech is the brake and reverse gear, *(see illustration)*. The only hill in the Skeldyke area is the 'Pullover', if it can be called a hill, that required a horse to sit in the breech to control farm vehicles as none of them had any brakes. To reverse a vehicle with shafts entailed the horse stepping backward pushing in the breech with its hindquarters.

Not having access to a tumbrel, but to give the reader some idea of the size to the best of my memory, it was like an open box, approximately four feet square and eighteen inches deep. This was supported some two feet from the ground on four stout wooden legs. Although extremely heavy, it was portable and used where animals required feeding in crew yards and out in the fields.

Horses are measured in hands, the width of a hand being recognised as four inches. A filly is a young female horse and becomes a mare when reaching adult life. A colt is a young male horse known as a gelding when castrated, most horses had this operation, a few were reprieved for breeding purposes.

Horse brasses were not so popular in the 1930's as they had been in earlier years. The only one I was familiar with was the face brass on the bridle, having them all over the harness must have been quite a chore to keep clean. I realise in these modern times horse brasses have become collectable items of which I have no information. I am aware there are displays in various Museums, Mauthorpe Museum near Alford for example, have a spectacular display of over seven hundred brasses.

One perk father had in the late 1920's and early 30's was the use of a horse and trap, cars being few and far between. This he put to good use during summer months by transporting the family on two or three weekends to the 'Plough Inn' at Quadring Fen, the home of maternal grandparents and a distance of twelve/fourteen miles. These grandparents also raised a large family of seventeen children, so that on our weekend visits there was always plenty of aunts and uncles surrounding us, one aunt being very popular who had a sweet shop! The outward journey was on a Saturday afternoon after father had finished work at mid-day, the pony was turned loose in the paddock behind the pub and we returned home early Sunday evening.

An incident occurred on one outward journey when a lone car drew alongside the trap, the driver informed father in no uncertain manner that he was causing a nuisance and should get off the road. It would have been understandable if the trap was holding up a queue of traffic, but there wasn't another car in sight. Father managed to bite his tongue and it was the subject for serious discussion in the 'Plough' that night. It was eventually decided that all iron beasts should be banned from the road, this being the power of a few pints of good honest ale!

The pub was mainly the domain of the men, it was rare to see a woman enter a public house. The country hostelry was not very inviting for the feminine species anyway, the 'Boat and Gun' and the 'Plough Inn' were typical with only one public room. This was known as the 'Taproom', the name was derived, it is believed, when barrels were stored and tapped in the same room as the customer drank the beer. This was not so at the Plough Inn for example, where the barrel and bottle beer were kept in a cellar three or four steps down from where the beer was drank. This meant the beer was drawn from the barrel straight into the glass and carried up the steps to the customer in the taproom. A half-gallon jug was used when three or four pints of beer were required at the same time.

The atmosphere of a country pub was not all that inviting in the 1920's and 30's, there would be a blazing fire in the winter, but the floor was tiled and walls bare except for one or two beer adverts. Furniture consisted of wooden tables and bench type seats that were not very comfortable. Games available in the smoke filled room included darts, dominoes, cards and table skittles. As children, we were barred from the taproom during opening hours, but were allowed to play with the games when it was closed.

Pubs were prominent in the Fenlands of Lincolnshire prior to World War II, there were at least twenty-three within a three-mile radius of Kirton War Memorial, one would be within easy walking distance of any inhabitant in that area. Twelve are known to have closed, the remainder serving meals at reasonable prices, something unthinkable in the 1930's. One may wonder why there were so many pubs in this small area, I suppose travel was limited and pubs grew up around their houses. Then there was always the legacy of hostelries required by travellers of days gone by. Many were staging posts and later with the advent of the railways, hotels appeared adjacent to many stations, Kirton for example with the 'Great Northern', a popular pub, now demolished to make way for Pell's Drive in Station Road.

The Agricultural Wages Board determined the structure of wages as outlined for 1935 in Currency, Prices and Wages. By the time I left school in 1936 there had been an increase, my starting wage was 11s 4d (57p) for a forty-eight hour working week, there was extra payment for overtime and increases were automatic on attaining each birthday. Full wages for men were attained at twenty-one years of age, in 1936 the full wage was £1. 17s 0d (£1.85). However, I was awarded full wages at eighteen years of age that I suppose was an achievement. I had been working beside the men both in a gang and father with a team of horses. From the age of sixteen I was working with the men at piecework rates doing seasonal work and was paid equal share. What I can say is that the jobs were hard work and the money well earned. My first piecework job at the tender age of sixteen was stooking (the double 'oo' sounded like 'ou' as in stout, stouking) one Saturday afternoon in a forty-acre field. Although I was favoured by having the inside turn, that is the two shortest rows, I still thought the team was trying to kill me! They were not of course, they were extremely helpful. Of all the piecework jobs in which I was involved, the hardest has to be cutting mustard seed. The method was known as 'hawming', the left arm gathering enough of the stalks to make a sheaf and the right hand cut them free at the base with a sickle. The sheaf was then pulled free and tied with string.

The normal working day started at seven in the morning to four in the afternoon with just a half-hour break at eleven o'clock. As we usually worked some distance from home it was the custom to have a packed lunch. The typical farm worker type of packed lunch was one thick piece of white bread, I never saw brown bread until many years later, with a large slice of beef, fat bacon or cheese. Every one carried a pocket-knife that might be used for all sorts of things during the morning. Then at lunchtime the knife would get a quick wipe on a trouser leg and used to cut a corner off the bread to use as a thumb piece to hold the meat or cheese. The knife would then continue to be used to cut slices as required. For some men that was the whole lunch, but father followed with a large jam pasty or slice of slab cake. Mother was an excellent cook, both the pasty and slab cake was cheap to make and particularly good when hot.

As a boy of fourteen I was aware of father's typical lunch and mother was aware that type of lunch wouldn't suit me, so she packed me some very dainty sandwiches with small pieces of cake and pasty. As soon as I opened my lunch box on that first day the 'leg pulling' started that continued for a few days, much to my embarrassment. Thermos flasks were popular at that time but very fragile, tea was the normal drink, I don't remember anyone ever having coffee. I knew that father liked to carry a bottle of cold tea with him in the summer with no milk or sugar that I didn't relish. However, I soon learned during that first summer out in the fields working under a hot sun, cold tea is a good thirst quencher. A tip worth remembering!

Toilet facilities was none existent, when working near one of the farms the crew yards were the obvious choice. It was different out in the fields, bearing in mind we were often working in the company of women, but dykes and hedges proved very useful.

Hygiene was not a high priority, water was rarely available anyway. Inquiring about hands being washed before lunch brought a wry smile to the faces of my fellow seasoned workers. They replied that I was going to eat a peck of muck during my lifetime so I might as well get started. No sympathy just another lesson learned the hard way.

*Incidentally in a February 2000 newspaper, experts were saying that grime is good for us. Our homes are too clean and we wash our hands too often. Perhaps it was good advice I was given after all, that has taken experts over sixty years to find out!*

Dirt never seemed to do us any harm anyway, no matter how dirty our hands were they merely got a wipe on an hessian sack. I think the worst time was once riddling 'tates' and having to throw an enormous amount of rotten ones into the trench, but we survived even that episode without any health problems.

We were sitting on a dyke bank one beautiful summer's day preparing to eat lunch, with a clear blue sky and larks soaring high overhead. Beside me was George Ashwell, affectionately known as 'Bunk' and a true Fenlander who picked some young dandelion leaves that were growing close by, he laid them on his fat bacon and ate them like lettuce. Encouraged to try this succulent plant, which I had been feeding to my rabbits for a number of years, I found the leaves to be tasty and often used them in my sandwiches. A word of warning though, I would not recommend eating them today without being thoroughly washed, also to wash the leaves and flower thoroughly before feeding them to rabbits. Having savoured young dandelion leaves that I know can be eaten like lettuce, I have not tasted dandelion wine, but have been told it is excellent. Recipes are available in most cookery books.

Diseases that have plagued British cattle in recent years were unheard of in the 1930's, at least that I was aware of. In the summer months cattle lazily ate luscious green grass in the fields then laid down to chew the cud. In the winter they were housed in warm crew-yards and fed a staple diet of wheat chaff, chopped mangolds, pulp and linseed cake. The pulp was a by-product produced at the factory from sugar beet and delivered to the farm in huge hessian sacks. The pulp was therefore sweet that gave the mundane diet a taste the cattle enjoyed. This produced some fine prime beef local butchers were pleased to sell in their shops.

One cow was always given special treatment that provided milk twice daily for the foreman and some of the workers. We were fascinated in our boyhood days to watch the milking process by hand, no doubt termed to be old fashioned today. The taste of fresh milk from the bucket, or even being squirted straight from the teat into our mouths, was refreshing to say the least. The first milk from a cow after a calf is born is known as beastlings - sounds like 'beslings' - which was thick, creamy and taste delicious. Many of us drank gallons of milk straight from the cow that did us no harm, but I wonder if the authorities would allow such a milking and drinking process today?

Cattle trucks were few and far between, the cattle would therefore be driven on the road to Boston for example. I only assisted the garthman a couple of times to drive some eighteen/twenty exuberant beasts to market. Although we had cycles with us, they were not much use on the outward journey, those beasts had no idea of the route and ran all over fields and gardens, it was akin to a cross-country run. We did stop at the 'Ship Inn' on London Road on the way home to eat a packed lunch, which I thought might be a bonus. The garthman liked his pint of ale, but being under-age I had to be content with a mineral.

There were no small gauge railway lines in Skeldyke, these were installed on farms where fields were a long way from a tarmac road, the small trucks pulled by horses. The nearest small gauge line that was almost a mile long was to the south of Skeldyke School at Lammings Marsh. There was a much longer line to the north of the school installed at Manor Farm on Sandholme Lane. W. Dennis and Sons built both lines before the First World War, and I understand they ceased operating about the middle of the Second World War.

Where there are horses there are blacksmiths. With such a density of horses in the Fens there was no less than eleven blacksmith shops within a three-mile radius of the village of Kirton, two of them were in the Skeldyke. If my memory serves me right, the one at the 'Boat and Gun' had a visiting blacksmith perhaps one or two days a week. Whereas at Burton House Farm owned by Ralph Tunnard, the blacksmith shop employed two full-time skilled craftsmen, who made and fitted iron shoes to the feet of horses of all shapes and sizes. It may not be widely known that shoes were not fitted to the back feet of horses that worked daily in the fields. When shoes were fitted to the front feet of a horse, the back feet would be trimmed, similar to cutting one's own toe nails. Shoes would only be fitted to the back feet of those horses who were continually working on the road. To be kicked by one of those iron-shod feet would have the recipient hopping about for a few days. I didn't heed the warning and suffered the pain, learning once again to listen to the advice of the wise men!

The farm blacksmith not only had to shoe horses, but there were all the implements that required repairs. Drag and harrow tines and plough shares needed sharpening. From time to time, particularly in a dry season, tines and shares were often worn so much that pieces had to be welded on them to restore them to their original size. The building used by a blacksmith would be known as 'The Forge', but often referred to as a 'Blacksmith Shop'. The reason for the last name must have been due to all the hand tools that were on display. Spades, shovels, various forks, hoes of all sizes, beet and hedging knives, a scythe, the tool often referred to as a 'man killer', just to name a few that were sold by the blacksmith.

The blacksmith's shop was a hive of industry, the hammer hitting hot metal two or three times with a couple of hits on the anvil while the smithy studied the shape made fascinating sounds. The bellows increasing the draught to keep a red-hot fire in the centre of the furnace to heat the iron. My father trying to keep two or three horses quiet while the blacksmith fitted new shoes, all very fascinating to a young lad. The shop was the focal point for visitors and the source of gossip, or should that be 'local information'. All that changed when the farm was sold and the blacksmith shop closed in the 1930's. The big black building still stands on the side of Nidds Lane used mainly I believe for farm storage.

Moving away from horses, steam engines were prominent in those years. Threshing sets comprising of drum, elevator and either a chaff cutter or hay press, were hauled and driven by a steam engine was a common sight. This was another attraction for young lads watching a threshing operation with the steam engine puffing away and blowing out surplus steam. Although I was fortunate not to be involved, the most frustrating job for a youth - and the job has been known to be done by a woman - was supplying water to a steam engine. Water would be obtained from a nearby drain and carried in two buckets suspended on chains from a yoke across the shoulders. The water was stored in a large tub and when full the lad, or woman, expected to have gained a few minutes respite.

But no such luck, the crafty engine driver, however, was waiting for this moment, as soon as the person had turned their back all the water was siphoned out of the tub. The whole operation having to be done all over again by whoever was carrying the water. Why do we do things supposed to be in fun that turns out to be so cruel?

A steam cultivating set comprised of two mighty engines each weighing around nineteen ton when fully laden with coal and water, a four furrowed two way plough, a heavy duty cultivating drag, water bowser and a living van. One engine would be positioned at each end of a field and pull the plough between them by means of a steal hawser operated from a turntable underneath the engine. They were a delight to observe, again as a boy, seeing them puffing away using the steam whistle to signal between the two drivers.

Steam power was used in the spreading of stone chipping on the road. The local council operated two steam lorries that distributed the stone depositing it in heaps beside the road along with barrels of tar. These huge barrels of tar would be hauled up by a system of pulleys to be poured into a cauldron supported on four iron wheels pulled by a horse. The tar was heated by means of a coal fire under the cauldron, then the very hot tar was sprayed on the road surface and covered by the stone that was spread by three or four men with large shovels and barrows. Finally a steam roller weighing twelve ton would travel over the surface two or three times pressing the stone into the tar giving the road a new surface. At night the horse would be turned loose in a grass field loaned by a local farmer and the steamroller would be parked on a suitable piece of roadside, the driver sleeping in the van. This was a type of caravan built of thick heavy wood on four wooden wheels. An example can be seen at Lincolnshire Life Museum at Lincoln.

Steam trains passed through Kirton Station from 1848 until closed in 1970. During that period of 122 years it was an extremely busy station and a focal point of the village. Kirton Station was situated between the towns of Boston and Spalding on the Grimsby to Peterborough London North Eastern Railway (LNER). The staff consisted of stationmaster, clerks, porters, a team of at least three men operated the signal box in Station Road, there was a gatekeeper in King Street, and in the latter years there was a lorry driver complete with lorry.

This was a busy goods yard and in the height of a season such as potatoes and sugar beet, at least seventy or eighty trucks would be dispatched to various destinations. Other goods going out were fresh vegetables, fruit, corn and cattle. Incoming goods included seed potatoes mainly from Scotland, fertilisers, coal and livestock. There were a number of merchant's offices in the station yard dealing with the movement of all these goods. Most working days there would be a small shunting engine from Boston moving trucks in and out of the yard. This caused huge hold-ups on Station Road because the crossing gates would be closed for long periods.

Living on the Skeldyke side of the railway line often meant we were held at the crossing gates when going to and from the village. Again as a young lad it was fascinating to witness the shunting process, then the main line would be cleared to let an express train go thundering through unhindered. Next was to marvel at a goods engine slowly passing by hauling one hundred or more heavy-laden trucks, wondering how they derived so much energy from coal and water, proving the power of steam is tremendous!

During my days on the farm from 1936 to 1941, I was often at the station delivering or collecting goods with horse drawn vehicles. I soon found out that steam engines and horses were not compatible, so there was often some tense moments keeping the horses under control when a steam engine was in the vicinity. Express trains did not amuse them and those horses that father fed were full of energy making the job very difficult. Fortunately one of the porters was a school chum and had been born on a farm, so he often came to my rescue. A young inexperienced horse would need an extra pair of hands anyway. Even when it was harnessed between two mature horses it would tremble and sweat profusely. Three or four visits were needed to get it in a calmer frame of mind.

In the early 1930's an innovation, a Gyrotiller, appeared cultivating the fields in the Kirton Marsh area. This was a huge track machine with a wheel in the front and two rotating cultivators at the rear and was larger than any tractor (see illustration). It was powered by a 180-hp diesel engine that had a fuel consumption averaging six gallons per hour. The working speed averaged one mile per hour at depths from fifteen to twenty inches covering a width of ten feet. The machine was not popular in this area, as father remarked, it was working too deep uncovering sub-soil and damaged drainage pipes. The Gyrotiller is known to have done an enormous amount of work in other parts of Great Britain, and proved popular in France, West Indies, Africa and India.

Tractors in the late 1920's and through the 30's started to make their mark! This was to the detriment and disgust of horsemen, who saw their work with horses being eroded. Their remarks being horses would always be required on the farm, therefore they would never be dispensed with completely. Yet at that time, for example, if a tractor ploughed ten acres in a working day, it would have required ten teams of horses and ten men to have completed the same amount of work. Other comparisons could easily be made, hence the reason tractors and mechanical machinery dominate farms today, easily doing all the tasks undertaken by horses, and probably a lot more. We have therefore seen the demise of the farm horse, unfortunately there has been a large reduction in full-time farm labour, but in turn has created the modern trend of gangs doing seasonal work.

It was at the tender age of six that I was introduced to my first bike (cycle) that was a second hand model purchased from a neighbour and I was briefly introduced to it on the first evening. Next day at the school lunch break, some pals offered to help in the hope they might have the opportunity of riding it themselves. The bike was held steady while I mounted and travelled a few yards. Despite my protest I was released to proceed on my own, immediately lost control and headed straight into the dyke beside the road. The bike was alright but my right arm was severely damaged resulting in me staying at home that afternoon.

There was an inquest around the tea table that night and Mr. Ralph Tunnard, father's boss, was contacted to see if he would transport us to Wainfleet to see Mr. Barton, a well-respected old-fashioned bonesetter. Mr. Tunnard agreed and cancelled a meeting in Boston to carry out the request. Now riding in a motor car in 1928 was real luxury, but I was in no mood to enjoy the occasion.

In answer to the knock on the door on arriving in Wainfleet, a gentleman with a lovely white beard who was Mr. Barton opened it. We were ushered into the parlour and introduced to Mrs. Barton, I estimated the couple to be aged in their seventies. Mr. Barton diagnosed a broken arm and proceeded to repair the damage and then bandage it with cardboard splints. Instructions that were given to father were duly passed to mother, that a cold cabbage leaf was to be placed on the arm every night for two weeks. As the accident happened in November those leaves could not have been colder, the other instruction was even worse, on arrival home I was to be given a tablespoonful of castor oil. 'For what reason?' I asked, and was told it calmed the nerves, I've never liked the stuff since. On the way home that night the car stopped at a pub in Wrangle, it seemed the two men wanted something to calm their nerves!

At the end of the two-week period the bandage was discarded and the use of those cold leaves abandoned. Then there was another problem, my arm was bent and very weak, causing mother a certain amount of worry. To the rescue came Miss. Cumberworth, a school teacher and qualified Red Cross Nurse, who suggested exercising with a weight, the flat iron therefore found another use besides ironing clothes. Every night for a month mother made me exercise with the iron, although agony at the time, it proved successful and the arm returned to normal. This was an extraordinary piece of physiotherapy that didn't cost a penny! The cost of Mr. Barton's services was only 2s 6d, (2/6 or 12½p in today's currency) the 'taxi' was free, the latter being all part of the Skeldyke community spirit, as also was Miss. Cumberworth's advice.

Eighteen months later playing football in the school playground, a game of which I have no interest, I damaged my left arm when I fell, or was I tripped? The inquest at the tea table resulted in two days passing before it was decided I should pay Mr. Barton another visit. Mr. Tunnard again freely supplying the transport, a fractured arm was diagnosed and the procedure was the same as before, cardboard splints, cold cabbage leaves and the dreaded castor oil that tasted no better. On the way home the car stopped at Wrangle for the two men to have their medicinal drink!

After the two-week period the bandage was discarded and the month of agony began with the flat iron exercise, that again proved successful. Despite the unorthodox treatment, neither arm has ever caused me problems, nor in my teens when I could easily lift unorthodox weights mentioned in another part of the Skeldyke story.

Mr. Barton's expertise has been included to highlight the old fashioned bonesetters as being a rare breed of people who are a great help to society. They may not have any formal medical qualifications but are capable of mending broken bones and dislocated limbs. I have found them very professional in giving me a valuable service over many years, it's a gift they have for which I am most grateful. As my current bonesetter tells me, he doesn't know all the medical terms, but he knows where everything fits, and that is good enough for me.

Bikes were my main means of transport through school days and my youth, as already mentioned I started riding a second-hand model at the age of six, this was passed to my sister when I was given a bigger one. My first new bike was purchased at the age of fourteen from Joe Fox, who had a cycle shop in Kirton. It was an ordinary Hercules model that cost £4.19s.11d. paid for with money earned in school holidays. Then in August 1939 I paid twelve guineas cash (£12.12s.0d or £12.60 in today's currency) for a 'Rolls Royce' bike, a Sunbeam, purchased from Walker's cycle shop in High Street, Boston. It was one of the first bikes to be equipped with calliper brakes, also included in the price was Sturmy-Archer three speed gears, an oil bath chain case and a dynamo.

Referring to school days, the sign above the left-hand entrance to the demolished school in Marsh Road, Skeldyke, read: 'Boarding School for Infants'. No date was found on the school when it was built, but had the appearance of being in two parts, the infant part looking very old, perhaps middle nineteenth century! When I joined the school at the age of four in 1926, there were three teachers each with classes of around thirty pupils. It was at this school that I received my total elementary education, leaving after ten years at the age of fourteen. During those ten years I found school most uninteresting and still refer to them as a life sentence, it was not a favourite period of my life.

A cousin who was a few years older than me, almost says the same thing in his autobiography, he left school at the age of fourteen and through his own efforts went on to be a successful self-employed accountant. My son Keith preferred leaving the local Secondary Modern School at the age of fifteen. Although having a chequered career, he eventually obtained through his own efforts a 'Bachelor of Horticultural Science Degree' and even married an attractive Australian school teacher.

On reflection, the teaching standards must have been high at the Marsh School, because many pupils went on to the Grammar and High Schools in Boston, then to Universities. I was pleased that my youngest brother joined these ranks, attending Grammar School and graduating to Newcastle University where he obtained a 'Bachelor of Science Degree'. No doubt there are others who have similar stories of graduating from this school in the 'Sticks' and obtaining various degrees. I think therefore the old adage applies, 'You can lead a horse to water, but you can't make him drink when you get him there', and I certainly didn't want to drink! But as my own career suggests, and the two mentioned in the above paragraph illustrates, talents may lie dormant with no effort being made in learning as a child, but those talents will eventually emerge and the child will find its niche in society in adult life.

As I was determined to leave school at the age of fourteen, I bluntly refused to take the eleven-plus examination, much to the consternation of my teachers. They tried to convince me I would easily pass and so enter life at the Grammar School, a direction I had no intention of pursuing. First of all I didn't think my parents could afford the cost and secondly I would be more use to them earning some extra cash. Having been earning money in the school holidays picking 'tates' for example, I wanted to get out on the farm in a full-time job. Incidentally I say 'tates' and 'bikes' because as a lad I never knew them to be called anything else, potatoes, cycles or bicycles, surely they were foreign words!

At school I somehow managed to obtain the dizzy heights of being one of two head boys. I'm still not sure if this was an honour or punishment, as we copped for such jobs as keeping the coal buckets full and fires well stoked. Should a fire go out, then we had to light it and they were not easy to get started. There was also washing the headmaster's car and going with him to measure land for local farmers. Our job was to pull the measuring chain marking each length with a metal stake. This did enable us to do a spot of scrounging, proving I learned something that was useful when I joined the RAF.

The privies were the bucket types in brick cubicles at the back of the school, boys were partitioned off from the girls, the brick building can be seen in the photograph later in the book. In my humble opinion this type of toilet facility was less hygienic than our wooden seat and vault at home. Washing hands was never a priority, there was no running water anyway. The only water available was drawn up in a bucket from the cistern sunk in the playground. There was a pump in front of the school but its main function was to assist us to climb onto the roof to retrieve any balls that were lodged behind the middle chimney.

The school garden was divided into plots, two boys being allocated to each one. Teaching us gardening was like another old adage: 'Teaching grandmother to suck eggs'. Living in the country, as we did, most of us were gardening at home, perhaps not always by choice. It was a chore I didn't mind, so father, who didn't have the time to do the work, was teaching me the art, plus grandfather was an excellent teacher.

Returning to school one day after a lunch break, four or five of us were alleged to have been chasing bullocks in a nearby grass field. We were duly paraded in front of the class and, surprise, surprise, we were offered a choice of punishment. We could accept the headmaster's form that was the cane across the bare hands, or be punished by the farm foreman. I opted to see the foreman whom I knew was a reasonable man and it transpired that he was not available, that pleased us all immensely. When the foreman eventually learned of the incident, he immediately dismissed it, so we escaped any punishment. We were not guilty anyway, because as the foreman was well aware, when a storm is imminent, as it was that day, bullocks will chase around the field kicking up their heels of their own accord.

However, the foreman did turn a blind eye to two crimes we were committing, trespassing and pinching bird's eggs. Perhaps he was remembering his boyhood days!

I reluctantly played a bit of football and cricket, the whip and top and marbles were more my scene, they were not so energetic. Collecting cigarette cards were prominent with all the boys. The series included wild animals; dogs; chickens; birds; butterflies; horses; fish; cars and flowers, just to name a few, it was a hobby that proved to be interesting and educational. But why did those last two or three cards in each series take so much finding that became so frustrating?

It wasn't customary for mothers to escort their brood to school, this honour was bestowed on an elder brother or sister, or an elder child of a neighbour. There were no school buses in the 1920's, so children walked long distances of at least two or three miles from such places as: Bowser's, Kirton and Lammings Marshes, Seadyke, Bucklegate and Frampton. Bikes were few and far between that were actually a luxury for many families.

Outings were also a luxury for many of us, I was fortunate to go on two organised by the school. The first was by coach to Whipsnade Zoo soon after it opened, I always remember there being two drivers, the same journey today would easily be done by one man. The second was a day trip by train to London that proved an exhilarating experience. Every Christmas we were taken by bus to join the Kirton school for tea in the Town Hall provided by the 'Buffs'. (The Antediluvian Order of the Buffaloes). We also received with the tea an apple, orange and a few sweets, then were entertained by local people. In the latter years at school, after the tea in the Town Hall, we were taken to a cinema in Boston, believed to be the New Theatre, where I saw my first film.

In 1935 the Silver Jubilee of King George V and Queen Mary was celebrated with a Gala in Kirton. The Skeldyke School joined Kirton in a fancy dress competition. A parade from the Town Hall headed by the village Brass Band consisted of decorated bikes, perambulators and all of us who had entered the fancy dress. We marched to the football field in Willerton Road and on arrival the fancy dress competition was judged which came out in favour of our school. This list names the winners but not in winning order.

**Girls over the age of ten:**

| | |
|---|---|
| Emma Housam | Gypsy |
| Muriel Dawson | McDougall's |
| Gwendolyn Naylor | Mary Mary Quite Contrary |

**Boys over the age of ten:**

| | |
|---|---|
| Jim Cook | Fagged Out |
| Richard Loveday | Fisherman |
| Joe Hilton | Chimney Sweep |
| Stanley Naylor | Pastry Cook |

The problem with being Pastry Cook was looking after those delicious fruit pies. They not only tended to wilt in the extreme heat, but it was a job keeping them away from sticky fingers! However, after the group photograph had been taken, displayed later in the book, those pies proved to be just as good as they looked.

During school holidays besides picking 'tates', I had the prestigious job of pig tenting. After the harvest was cleared, we were permitted to glean the loose corn to feed our chickens. Some of the fields where a lot of corn was on the ground, a herd of pigs would be turned loose to do some scavenging. It was my job to keep them in the field allotted to them and this was easy when corn was plentiful. Then one very hot day after enjoying my lunch I fell asleep, which the pigs were quick to take advantage of. This caused me problems, I got the pigs back in the corn field, but couldn't hide the rooting they had done in the 'tatie' field, that resulted in getting my wrists slapped.

One instruction I received still has me puzzled, that was to keep the pigs away from water. 'For what reason?', I asked and was told that when they swim they cut their throats with their front feet. On reflection I don't recall there ever been any water near the field, had the pigs been inclined to have a swim. As boys we were always getting our 'leg pulled'. One example when in a field at the far end of the farm erecting posts, we would be asked to go to the yard and fetch a load of post-holes. The pig story could well be in this category, unless someone knows different?

In the early 1930's there was a group of lads my age who were regular beaters for shooting parties organised on Saturdays by local farmers during the winter. Three or four men with dogs would join us to trail over ploughed fields and through crops disturbing pheasants, partridges, hares and rabbits for the sport of men with guns.

There were a few hair-raising incidents where hares and rabbits were shot only a few paces in front of us, birds were shot just over our heads dropping almost at our feet. On one occasion pellets peppered the side of our transport, fortunately we were not on board. *(As I write this I am wondering whether we were being trained for World War II which we didn't know was only a few years in the not too distant future. Perhaps that is being facetious).*

Our monetary payment was 2s.6d (2/6 or 12¹/₂p) that was a small fortune at that time and well worth all the hard work walking over muddy fields. We also received a cold lunch of pork pie, dough cake and cheese, all very tasty, but washed down with ice-cold minerals. A steaming hot cup of tea would have been most welcomed.

Garthmen cooked 'tates' for the pigs in a huge copper that would be piled high covered with wet sacks. With a bit of 'cloak and dagger' effort making sure the 'tates' were cooked and the garthman out of sight, several hands would be grabbing the biggest available. Well they tasted better than what mother cooked, and perhaps it was 'pigs' that ate them after all!

Built in 1908, the Primitive Methodist Chapel is north of the school and was very popular in the 1920's and 30's. It was a ritual on a Sunday morning that we attended Chapel from 11.00 am to 12.00 noon. Then at night I would attend the service with grandmother. Those straight back wooden seats were not very comfortable and got worse if it was a long sermon. Should grandmother not be attending Chapel, then I had to accompany mother to the Mission Church, which was Church of England, so getting a mixed religion.

Naturally father was aware of this situation when I joined the RAF, he suggested that I should say my religion was C of E. 'For what reason?' I asked. 'There are not so many Methodists and they seem to get detailed for cookhouse duties', he replied. This proved to be a valuable piece of advice in the following years.

The Methodist anniversary took place on the first Sunday in June, with a service both in the afternoon and evening. This was the time of year for new suits and frocks that put a strain on parents finances, but we had to look our best when reciting poetry or just reading pieces from the Bible.

There were perks for participating in the anniversary and for regular attendance on Sunday mornings. One was the annual prize giving, these were usually books that I for one very much appreciated.

The popular perk was the annual day trip to Skegness that involved the whole family. Father would harness a horse to a trolley on which was placed loose wooden seats to transport many families to Kirton Station. On arrival the horse would be turned loose in a field adjacent to the station, his perk for hauling us on the two-mile journey. Travelling on a passenger steam train just once a year was sheer luxury creating much excitement. Even parents, mine included, would never travel further than Boston from one year end to another, so a trip to Skegness was a real treat for them also.

The train travelled via Boston, Firsby and Wainfleet, to Skegness station that is in operation today, still catering for the day tripper and weekly holiday makers that visit this popular seaside resort. On leaving the station most families headed for the golden sandy beach that was always crowded. It was cheaper to play at making sand castles than touring the amusements and shops. We were always assured of a donkey ride and an ice cream, with a swim in the clear blue water of the North Sea being sheer pleasure compared to the murky water we were used to on Kirton Marsh. The only problem getting sun burnt was suffering an uncomfortable night or two in bed. As far as I am aware there was no fear of cancer that prevails today.

The highlight of the trip was tea in the Winter Gardens, free for children attending Sunday School, the parents chipping in to cover their own costs. Then it was back to the station and the return train journey to Kirton. Father had to catch the horse and harness it to the trolley, we then travelled back to Skeldyke sitting on those hard wooden seats, even that was better than walking. The trip was a talking point for many a long day, and the envy of those who had not joined the excursion.

Various events were organised by the Chapel hard working committee to raise the funds for the prizes and the trip to the seaside. The main one was a gala day held in the grass field adjacent to Ivy House that had the usual activities including skittles, bowling for a pig, bean board, children's fancy dress, decorated bikes, bouncing baby competition, not literally of course, plus other things designed to help the fund.

The Mission Church committee also organised a gala that took the same form as the Chapel, their venue was a grass field adjacent to Blossom

Hall. The main attraction at both events seemed to be bowling for a pig that brought participants in from surrounding villages. The final would often be played in the glare of car headlights, and there were not many cars around in those days.

One famous lady can be attributed to Kirton Skeldyke. Sarah Anne Swift was born in 1854 into the farming fraternity, believed to be on the Blossom Hall Estate, and she carved an awe-inspiring career in the nursing profession. Sarah joined the Dundee Royal Infirmary as a probationer and eventually graduated to Assistant Matron. There was a move to Liverpool and another to London where she was installed as the Night Supervisor in a fever hospital. This was followed with a period of studying American nursing in New York.

Returning to London, Sarah was appointed Assistant Matron at Guy's Hospital then moved on to be Lady Superintendent of the Trained Nurses Institute, a position she held until her retirement in 1909. Her retirement was short lived. At the outbreak of the First World War in 1914 Sarah was recalled to duty and appointed Matron-in-Charge of the Joint War Committee of the British Red Cross in the Order of St. John. She gave devoted service during the war years and for her stamina and drive was known as the 'Mighty Atom'. For her dedication the Lady of Grace of St. John of Jerusalem was bestowed on her and in 1919 she became Dame Grand Cross of the Order of the British Empire. After the war Dame Sarah founded the College of Nursing in London and died in 1937 at the age of eighty-three. She did not therefore see the College of Nursing given the honour of being named the Royal College of Nursing in 1946. Dame Sarah is remembered in the Lady Chapel in Kirton Church and a ward at Guy's hospital in London carries her name.

Not so famous as the above lady, but a familiar figure on the roads around Skeldyke was Tom Patman. Horses travelling on the roads everyday left an awful lot of 'muck' that is excellent manure for rhubarb beds, but it kept Tom busy two or three days every week trying to keep the roads clean. He also had the job of digging channels on the side of the road to drain off all the water that accumulated in large pools on the tarmac surface after a heavy rain. Then during the summer he had the tremendous hard work of swinging a scythe cutting a swathe of grass on each side of the road to keep the highway clear. When snow blocked the roads in the winter, Tom mustered a gang of men, usually farm workers who were unable to work on the land, who cleared the snow with shovels and brute strength.

Another familiar sight that traversed the roads twice a week in the 1920's and early 30's, was 'PERSEVERANCE'. The name is defined in the dictionary as 'holding a cause of action or repetitive activity'. 'Perseverance' was the carriers' cart that left Kirton on Wednesdays and Saturdays at 9.00 am travelling via the 'Boat and Gun' in Skeldyke carrying passengers and goods to Boston. The return journey started from the White Horse Hotel in West Street at 3.00 pm.

The age of 'Perseverance' is not known, it could be thirty or more years. The photo that can be seen later in the book is believed to have been taken in 1932 and an article appeared in the Guardian newspaper in 1935.

The first owner was a Mr. Guy that according to my grandmother was known as 'Daddy' Guy. Owners following him were a Mr. Marsdon and a Mr. Penny, all before my time. The last owner was Mr. Lawrence Richardson and the two horses that pulled the cart were Betsy and Daisy who knew every inch of the route and it was impossible for Lawrence to get them to pass any normal stop. Besides passengers, Lawrence conveyed goods, large articles were stowed on top of the cart. Boots and shoes were also collected on the inward journey and left at Mr. Herring's in High Street for repair and picked up on the outward journey.

Between the ages of nine and twelve, I had the experience of travelling on 'Perseverance' joining the vehicle at the 'Boat and Gun'. To the best of my memory the seats were fixed bench types, perhaps a bit hard even with some upholstery. The clip-clop of the horses feet could be heard some distance away and was music to the ears of waiting passengers, especially at stops where there was no shelter and it was raining, or an east wind was blowing across the flat Fen land fields in this Lincolnshire countryside. Incidentally an east wind is known as a lazy wind, referred to locally as: 'Going through you'. Meaning that such a wind penetrates one's clothes and therefore difficult to keep warm.

Around the latter years of the carriers' cart, Mr. Ray Garwell, haulage contractor, who transported various goods during the week for example potatoes, sugar beet, corn and coal, then added passengers to the list. On Saturday afternoon the lorry would be washed, a canopy fitted and some loose wooden seats placed underneath. Departure was from the 'Boat and Gun' at 6.00 pm. Return fare to Boston was 1s.0d (1/- or 5p in today's currency) the lorry parked at the 'Axe and Cleaver' in West Street, departing at 10.00 pm.

This is a true story of a passenger purchasing a chamber pot and filling it with some of the finest ale, perhaps it was May Fair when country lads had the tendency to make merry. Or another local term: 'Let their hair down!' However, on boarding the lorry with the pot full of ale, fellow passengers were invited to have a drink. Everyone refused this generous offer, much to the delight of the owner who drank the beer to the very last drop. Well the pot was new and it had never been used for the purpose it was intended.

Then in the mid 1930's Skeldyke was afforded luxury coach travel when the Cropley Brothers each purchased a twenty-nine seated coach *(see photo for similar models)*. Dolph named his the 'Safety Coach' and established a route on Wednesdays to Boston Market through the Skeldyke via the 'Boat and Gun'. Dolph took on the roll of the carriers' cart of carrying passengers and goods, large articles being stowed on top. Boots and shoes were also collected for repair at the High Street cobblers, the coach being parked in West Street. Departure was at 2.00 pm, repaired boots and shoes collected on leaving the town. The reason for departing at that time was to enable Dolph to complete the journey then proceed to a school to take children home that he had transported there in the morning.

Les Cropley named his coach the 'Blue Glider', taking the same route as Dolph, but on Saturdays. Les did not carry goods but established three journeys carrying passengers via the 'Boat and Gun' to Boston. I'm not sure of the exact times the bus passed through Skeldyke, but 2.00 pm - 4.00 pm and 6.00 pm will suffice. Some of the 2.00 pm passengers would be returning on the 6.00 pm journey, then the next return journey would be at 8.00 pm. The last bus departing at 10.00 pm from the entrance of the 'White Hart' near the Town Bridge, that often resulted in double the number of passengers being on board than there were seats.

This was ideal for courting couples, or even if they weren't courting, it created some warmth in the winter, as I don't remember the heaters being very efficient even if there were any at all. This excess passengers resulted in Les often doing a short run before 10.00 pm and the last bus leaving much later. Eventually a forty-one seated coach came into operation that relieved the situation.

I have no knowledge of any stagecoach operating in the Skeldyke area, so 'Perseverance' could well be the forerunner of passenger transport in this flat Fenland countryside. The covered lorry operated during the latter period of the carriers' cart, both of them an essential part of the community at that time. Eventually they both had to give way to progress, the small twenty-nine seated coaches were introduced barely two or three years before World War II. Progress continued, coaches got bigger and today we have the twelve metre luxury coaches that travel, not just to local seaside resorts, but to places all over the UK and beyond the English Channel.

Our main mode of transport to Boston as youths, weather permitting, was the trusty bike that was stored for a modest sum at Walker's Cycle Shop in High Street. Was it on purpose, or just coincidence? We would be leaving the town at the same time as the last bus and slip-stream it through the country lanes of Wyberton and Frampton to Skeldyke, much to the consternation of the driver. I certainly don't recommend this rather dangerous practice today. Yes, it was dangerous in our time, but more so today because these modern coaches travel faster and have very powerful air brakes.

Entertainment in the Skeldyke was very much a do-it-yourself operation, with whist drives, galas or garden fetes as they were often referred, concerts and day trips by coach being popular. Many homes were installing a wireless and we acquired our first model in the mid-thirties. As there was no electricity, the set was operated from an accumulator, (nothing to do with betting on horses) this was a wet electricity glass storage battery with a handle at the top. We had three, one in use, one in a shop at Kirton being charged and a spare. These accumulators were bulky and heavy, carrying a vessel in one hand and trying to control the bike with the other proved to be precarious, and frowned upon by the local 'friendly' bobby.

Skeldyke had a formidable football team, so I am told, who played their games in the grass field behind Ivy House. As I had, and still have not, any interest in football, I have therefore no further information.

Holidays did not feature in many farm workers calendar, at least not booking a holiday that meant travelling any distance. They were allowed a few days paid holiday and these would more often than not be spent at home. On the Wednesday of such a holiday they would visit Boston Market and think they had had a great day out! If they enjoyed wildfowling, they would spend a lot of time on Kirton Marsh, shooting a bird or two helped with the family budget.

When the Cropley Brothers arrived with their luxury coaches in the mid 1930's, it afforded the people of Skeldyke opportunities to travel. The seaside resorts of Skegness and Hunstanton became more accessible. In the winter months parties were organised to visit shows at the Embassy Theatre, Peterborough, the Christmas pantomime was very popular, not just with the children, the adults enjoyed the spectacular performances. I recall around the age of sixteen going with father to a British Legion (it didn't have the Royal status until many years later) County Rally at Cleethorpes. This was my first visit to this resort and was a fabulous day's outing. The men, however, seemed to use the Rally as an excuse for a pub-crawl, perhaps another occasion when they 'let their hair down!' It would also be a talking point in the 'Boat and Gun' for a few nights.

During the 1920's and early 30's there was Foster the butcher delivering meat with a horse and light cart every Friday, Jessops the bakers delivering bread at least twice a week with a horse and similar cart, Mr. Penny delivered fruit and vegetables with a horse and trolley on a Thursday. He wouldn't have a very good trade with the vegetables around Skeldyke, but he did have a good trade at the school, it was amazing how many monkey nuts could be purchased for a 1d. The horse and trolley delivering coal soon gave way to a lorry. The grocers, Co-Operative from Kirton and Whittaker's from Boston, always had vans. Popple's were Boston grocers who started with a horse and van and changed to a three wheel motor cycle van. It was the grocers who delivered paraffin, the essential ingredient for the lamps that provided the lighting. Paraffin was also used for cooking with the two and three burner Valor stoves, they were very popular in the summer, it saved lighting those black iron grates when heating was not required in the house.

I don't recall any milkman, simply because we purchased our milk from the farm at a nominal price. It was carried in a can with a tight lid that proved a challenge to see how many times the can could be swung over one's head. Then one day the lid must have been a bit loose and I lost all the milk, an exercise never to be repeated, the consequences did not bear contemplating had it happened a second time.

Ice cream was delivered on a 'Stop Me and Buy One' tricycle that changed to a motor bike and sidecar. The mail was delivered on a bike, as also were telegrams. Like the motor car, telephones were few and far between, so the telegram provided a useful service frequently used for family announcements. The telegram boy was not always a welcome sight, not only did they announce weddings and births, I thought I had better put that in the right order, but often announced a death.

On a lighter note, animals, birds, flowers and trees were all part of the countryside, these lists may not be complete but were known to me to be in the Skeldyke in the 1920's and 30's.

**Animals**: The worst of the animals has to be rats that are vermin and very destructive, they are hated by most people including me. Yet looking back it seems I have been involved with them on many occasions. We were pestered with them at the 'Huts', although never in the house, they did kill four or five young rabbits when I kept as many as thirty in my school days. There was a wheat stack that had stood in the farmyard a few months that was infested with the vermin. The men who removed the thatch remarked they would be surprised if there was any corn left to be threshed. A wire fence was erected around the stack and we lost count how many rats were caught. Then an incident happened in 1945 when I was staying overnight in barracks at Detmold in Germany. A group of us were returning from a night-out on the town and as we entered the darkened porch, one of the lads shouted something had run up his trouser leg. He was bundled into the lighted room and his trousers peeled off to discover the invading creature was a rat. Suffice is to say the rat was killed and no harm done to the victim. This was an instance where 'Yerks' would have prevented the creature getting any further than the calf of the leg, instead of the thigh, which this piece of vermin had done.

Rabbits and hares were in abundance and sought after to adorn the table as they made very tasty pies. Ferrets were used to explore rabbit burrows, my only experience with these furry animals was being in the company of cousins down Holbeach Marsh that proved very productive. A word of warning about burrows and holes in the ground, it is wise not to explore them with bare hands. Many animals are vicious when cornered, it is safer therefore to use a spade.

Stoats and weasels are carnivorous mammals with brownish fur. The stoat is the larger of the two with a black tipped tail. The weasel has a slender body and short legs and is understood to not be afraid of man. In defiance it will rear itself up on its hind legs, I know one that tried that trick and lost the battle!

Moles are also furry creatures that cause an enormous amount of damage to lawns; their work in the form of heaps of soil is visible in many grass fields.

Snakes are reptiles and I only ever saw two in Skeldyke, both grass snakes, that are understood to be harmless. A young lady in Australia giving a demonstration on snakes gave assurance that snakes prefer to slide away from the human species. It is only when they are cornered or trod on that they fight back. Hence the reason for her advice to wear a stout pair of boots when walking where snakes are known to exist. Even so I prefer to keep a safe distance.

I don't recall seeing or hearing of a fox being in the Skeldyke area. This is surprising because all the farms and many households had chickens that might have attracted them.

Britain's only spiny mammal is the humble hedgehog that was often seen in the area. There was the story of hedgehogs sucking milk from cows as they lay in grass fields chewing their cud. Not knowing anyone who witnessed this unique operation, makes me wonder if it is another of those 'leg pulling' stories!

Cows were seen of course, during summer months eating luscious green grass then lying down to chew the cud. This is the food they have regurgitated from the first stomach to the mouth and chewed again. There is an old adage, 'Chew the cud', meaning to ponder.

**Birds:** Mother Nature provides a huge aviary where birds can fly as free as the wind providing beauty and song to the countryside. This is a selection that inhabited the Skeldyke area in my youth, and may still be seen today.

Sparrows are the most common of which there are at least three types, hedge, tree and house, all three are songsters warbling away in their particular domain. Meadow pipits, wagtails both grey and yellow with various finches all adding their song to the chorus. Corn and reed buntings, yellowhammers, wrens, skylarks, thrushes and blackbirds adding both song and colour to the precious countryside. An old prophecy handed down from grandparents says that when a blackbird sits all day singing in a loud voice, it is the sign of rain.

The woodpecker could be heard, and seen tapping away at the bark of a tree, and the cuckoo would be flying from tree to tree with its two-note call. The latter is a European bird greyish in colour that arrives on these shores around April and departs in August. It is known to lay its eggs in other bird's nests because it is too lazy to make one of its own.

The scavenger has to be the starling. Throw scraps of food on the garden and the 'bush telegraph' clicks into action and hordes of them appear from all directions.

Seagulls would hover close to a team of horses ploughing in the winter and have picked up juicy worms from the freshly turned soil close to my heels. One problem with these huge birds flying overhead, their toilet habits were uncontrollable, something I learned first hand! These birds were known locally as 'Fosdyke Labourers', for which I have no real explanation, except at night they always flew in the direction of Fosdyke on the West Side of the Wash.

Rooks and crows building nests high in the trees herald a dry summer, likewise waterhens building nests close to the water. Should the nests be high above water and low in the trees, then it's the sign of stormy weather, or so the wise men tell us!

The red, red robin adds a splash of colour, especially sitting on a carpet of snow in the winter. The wise old owl would give an eerie hoot in the night and the nightingale would serenade the countryside, even though it was not 'Berkeley Square'.

Swallows and swifts arrive in the spring and are recognised by their pointed wings and forked tail. They are fascinating to observe as they dart about collecting material to build their nests in the eaves of buildings.

Plovers are marsh birds but often seen inland. Fields of greens are the prey of pigeons who are very destructive, hence the reason for using a gun to banish them in the hope of shooting enough for a pie!

A flock of geese easily finds a field of green corn in the winter and is the target of a lurking gunman, again another tasty dish. Poachers targeted pheasants and partridges, mainly for the table because it saved on buying meat. The male pheasant is a very attractive bird with colourful plumage and the best bird for the table. Not that I ever shot any of these birds, but I have a brother who was handy with a gun.

There were many domestic birds both in the farmyards and backyards of houses that included chickens, ducks, turkeys, geese and quail, fed mostly for home use.

Butterflies are not birds, but they add a lot of colour to the countryside flitting around the flowers and hedgerows. There is one that causes trouble, especially in gardens, the white species lays its eggs on cabbages producing caterpillars that devour the plants.

**Flowers:** Like football, flowers are not my speciality, so my wife, Vera, has had to point me in the right direction. This is a selection known to have been growing in the Skeldyke and may still adorn the fields and roadside today.

The daisy is the most common flower and first to spring to mind. Many hours were spent as children collecting the pink and white flowers to make endless chains. Meadow buttercups have a bright yellow flower and were a common sight amongst the daisies. Cowslips might be known as primroses, the lovely yellow flowers in a cluster, according to my grandmother, make excellent wine.

The dandelion has many uses. The flower is one of the first to appear in the countryside and one of the last to fade away. The plant is harvested extensively to feed rabbits, I have collected thousands and fed them direct to the animals. But I would suggest today the greenery be thoroughly washed before feeding this succulent plant to them, likewise before using the leaves in a salad. Young leaves are the best for salads, they are tender in April, May and June, after this period they develop a slightly bitter taste. Although I have never tried it and bucketfuls are needed, I understand the flower makes an excellent country wine. History informs me the Victorians dug up the roots in the autumn, dried them and crushed them into a powder that made a drink akin to coffee. But I have no evidence to support this information.

Red clover is not only a wild flower that decorates roadsides, but it was cultivated to feed horses. There is a white flower and both colours are a good source of nectar sought after by busy bees to make honey.

Even I easily identified snowdrops, violets, honeysuckle, bluebells and the bright red poppy that bloomed on the roadsides and on dyke banks. Perhaps not so easily identified were cat's ear, this has a small yellow flower that could be mistaken for the dandelion. Granny's bonnet has a blue flower perhaps known as columbine. Bird's foot has a yellow and orange flower that might be known as 'bacon and eggs'. Bird's eye is a blue flower, foxgloves tend to be more of a purple shade. Chickweed has a noticeable small white flower and the leaves can also be used in a salad, but I have no experience of eating them. Cornflower is a weed that has a lovely blue coloured flower. Fat hen was a nuisance in the garden, but it had a small pale green flower and the plant apparently has been used in the kitchen in years gone by, but I know not in what capacity.

**Trees:** There were an abundance of trees in the Skeldyke and Bucklegate that enhanced this Fenland countryside. Hawthorn was the most prominent with its magnificent white flower that appeared in April/May and produced bright red berries in October. These trees and bushes were easy to plash. The method was to cut halfway through a branch about three or so feet from the ground, the top half would then be bent over and the branches entwined held down by stakes. Grandfather Naylor was an expert in performing this operation that took place in the winter when the sap was supposed to be low. When the branches were all laid at the same level it formed a hedge that acted as a permanent fence around a grass field, for example. In the spring the hedge would produce a mass of green shoots that would be trimmed keeping the natural 'fence' neat and tidy.

Hawthorn hedges supported the prickly bramble briar that produced those lovely succulent black fruit, known simply as blackberries. Arms would get scratched picking this fruit that made pies and jam, proving the effort to be worthwhile.

There were many oak and ash trees in the area, the first is remembered mainly because of its acorns, but the ash had strange winged seeds. The willow tree favours growing near water and has narrow leaves with catkin type flowers. There was also an elder hedge along the stone lane beyond Ashwell's house, besides the one around grandfather's garden, that had to be cut every year, but I don't know what happened to the useful six/seven foot sticks, possibly burned. Walnut trees in Bucklegate that were and, I believe are still standing at the far end of the same lane as the elder hedge, drew the attention of boys our age group when the nuts were falling freely on the roadside.

As children living in the countryside we were close to nature with the facts of life all around us. There was always something happening in the reproduction cycle with piglets, lambs and calves being born, and in my case rabbits being born on a regular basis. Chickens laid their eggs wherever they could nest and the farm cat seemingly produced a brood overnight. The horse population was in decline so foals were not so common, at least that I was aware of.

Skeldyke was a close knit community in the 1920's and 30's that had a rare innocence. For example, a bike could be left safely anywhere and would not have moved an inch on the return of the owner with any personal belongings still intact. House doors were often left unlocked and no one, and I mean no one, would think of crossing the threshold.

69

Farm implements were stored safely in open sheds and left in open fields without fear of vandalism or theft.

We were a hardy species during that period before World War II. There was no central heating, electric blankets, washing machines, dishwashers, electric typewriters, word processors and wall-to-wall carpets. Computers were never heard of, chips were part of our piece and penn'orth - fish and chips - we purchased on a Saturday night after a visit to the cinema. Cars were indeed a luxury and no one ever flew in an aeroplane. I did witness an air display by Alan Cobham in the mid 1930's at the airfield on Boardsides, Boston, and since then I have travelled many thousands of miles in various aircraft.

Television was unheard of, although Karl Ferdinand Braun introduced a cathode tube in 1897. Then John Logie Baird of Scotland gave a demonstration of television in 1926. Therefore we never had a box in the corner churning out the horrors of war, murder and rape. We were in a cocoon in this Lincolnshire Fenland, the world outside seemed to be all innocence, friendly and peaceful.

This picture of the outside world was shattered on Friday 1st of September 1939 when a contingent of soldiers arrived from the London area complete with searchlight *(see photo)* and generator. They took up residence in a field adjacent to 'The Pullover' on Marsh Road, barely half-mile from the well-populated school. Then two days later, on the 3rd of September 1939, we were at war with Germany that was to continue until 1945.

More soldiers arrived later as did evacuees from London and Hull, the latter were housed with families throughout the area. Mother received a family from London who became firm friends. Many of us who had been together from school days, left the sanctuary of our home environment and were landed in places around the globe we never knew existed. But that is another story!

The following are hand tools that I used in the late thirties during my apprenticeship on the farm, some of them are still in use in the garden in this year 2000.

**Sugar Beet Hoe:** Used to single plants left in clumps. It is 15 inches long with a swan neck, wooden handle and a 4.5 inch blade.

**Rub Stone:** Best described as a round grind stone, thicker in the middle than at the ends. 12 inches in length it is used to sharpen scythes and sickles.

**Carborundom:** Flat wet stone used to sharpen hedging and household knives, 9.5 inches long.

**File:** A hardened steel tool ridged surfaces used to sharpen knives on reapers and binders. 8.5 inches long, 4.5 inch wooden handle.

**Hand Fork**: There are two round tines 11 inches in length with a 47 inch wooden handle. Used for many things including loose straw and hay.

**Muck Fork:** Muck the farm name for manure. The fork has four round tines 13 inches in length and a width of 8 inches, the wooden 'T' shaped handle is 31 inches long.

**Metal Pan Shovel:** The pan is 11 inches deep and 10 inches wide with a 'T' shaped 28 inch wooden handle.

**Lyndon Spade:** The blade is 10 inches deep and 7 inches wide with a 'T' shaped 31 inch wooden handle.

**Planting Tool**: It has a blade 6 inches deep and 4 inches wide with an 8 inch 'T' shaped wooden handle.

**Tatie Fork**: 'Tatie' being the farm jargon for potato. The fork has four steel tines bevelled at the back. They are 11 inches long and 0.75 inches wide with a total width of 8 inches. The 'T' shaped wooden handle is 31 inches long.

**Hoe:** The handle is straight and 66 inches long, with interchangeable blades in varying shapes and sizes.

**Small Rake:** This has ten 2 inch long tines with a total width of 9.5 inches attached to a straight 48 inch long wooden handle.

**Large Rake:** This tool also has ten tines, they are 3 inches long with a width of 18 inches on a straight 35 inch long wooden handle.

**Scythe:** This tool is known on the farm as a 'Man killer', not literally, of course. I can vouch for it being a tool that involves some very back-breaking hard work. See the photograph of Mr. Ashwell giving a demonstration. The worst crop I ever cut was tares, they were all tangled and very heavy.

The scythe has a curved wooden handle with two handgrips. Comfortable settings for me are 9 inches from the top for the left-hand and 32 inches from the bottom for the right-hand. The curved 30 inch steel blade is 3 inches deep at the heel tapering to a point.

Most hand tools can be seen in farm museums, see back pages for locations.

As a boy I was astonished to see workmen spitting on their hands when using tools, my father and grandfather included, but I was never informed for what reason. However, on leaving school and joining the workmen using these hand tools, I soon learned how vital it was to use the spit. It was a method I soon adopted because it moistened the palms and helped to prevent too many blisters. Another farming tip is to keep the wooden handles well oiled, linseed oil is preferred, but clean lubricating oil is a good second best. Both oils keep the handles smooth and so are not rough on the hands.

# HARVEST

Blades of green corn herald the Spring,
    Wheat, barley and oats are the growing thing,
I gaze in amazement through rose tinted glasses,
    Seeing those acres producing food for the masses.

Early morning dew shining on a blanket of green,
    Sunshine enhancing the breathtaking scene.
Rain falling gently on the precious corn,
    The east wind making it all so forlorn.

After months of toil and tender care,
    Fields of yellow corn hail the Summer, so fair.
Golden wheat wafting gently in the breeze,
    Silken barley blending with the trees green leaves.

Autumn, the season of beauty that glows,
    This miracle achievement in the crops that grow.
Colours deepen as the  evening falls in the glade,
    In the shadows wild shapes are made.

Buntings flitting amongst the ears of corn,
    Field mice feeding, their right when born.
Pheasants, rabbits and hares in the corn unseen,
    Each one part of the harvest scene.

Wheat grown for the bread of life,
    Barley brewed for the beer that is rife.
Oats, the traditional food of the horse,
    All ingredients for the bumper harvest, of course.

The old fashion binder tying the sheaves,
    The threshing drum separating the corn with ease,
Everything gathered in unheeded,
    The harvest completed so crucially needed.

© *Stanley Naylor*

# PROFILE OF HORSE AND HARNESS

**BRIDLE:** This was fitted over the head and used to control the horse. A steel bit fits into the mouth with a rein from each side long enough to reach the driver sitting on a vehicle or in the case of implements they had to reach to the back of them. Blinkers (winkers) were fitted to the bridle so the horse would not be startled by anything on either side and therefore the horse can only see straight ahead. A piece of brass is usually fitted to the bridle on the forehead.

**COLLAR:** The bottom of the collar, being the widest part, has to fit over the top of the horse's head and ears, that being the widest part of the head. Hence the reason for the collar being put on and taken off upside down. The collar is turned on the neck as close to the head as possible, then fitted snugly against the shoulders. It is from the shoulders that the horse transmits it's enormous pulling power. It was recognised that in a field a horse could haul a ton on a two-wheeled cart, on the road it would be one and a quarter tons. On a four wheeled trolley fitted with rubber tyres the weight could go to one and a half tons, the maximum known was one ton thirteen hundredweights. The hames are made of steel and fitted the collar to which the chains are attached from the cart, trolley or implement.

**SADDLE:** This fits snugly on the horses back and takes the weight of the shafts of a two wheeled cart and part of the load. On top of the saddle is a steel channel over which passes a chain from the two shafts of the cart, trolley or wagon. The art of loading a cart therefore was to balance the weight on the two wheels there being no weight on the horse's back when hauling a four wheeled trolley/wagon or other implements. The girth strap has to fit tight to keep the saddle in place.

**BREECH:** This is the back part of the harness that fits under the tail and at the top of the legs. This piece of the harness enables a horse to reverse a cart, trolley, wagon or anything fitted with shafts. The breech also enabled the horse to act as a brake, there being no brakes fitted to farm vehicles. The straps going over the back of the horse is to keep the breech in place.

# HARNESS WORN BY FARM HORSES

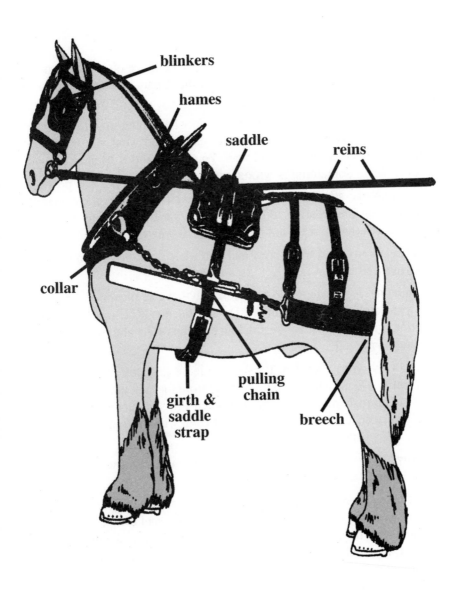

blinkers

hames

saddle

reins

collar

girth &
saddle
strap

pulling
chain

breech

# THE HORSE'S PRAYER

'To Thee, My Master, I Offer My Prayer'.

'Feed me, water and care for me, and, when the day's work is done, provide me with shelter, a clean dry bed, and stall wide enough for me to lie down in comfort.

Be always gentle with me, and talk to me. Your voice often means more to me than the reins. Pet me sometimes, that I may serve you the more gladly and learn to love you.

Do not jerk the reins, and do not whip me when going up a hill. Never strike, beat, or kick me when I do not understand what you mean, but give me a chance to understand you. Watch me, and if I fail to do your bidding, see if something is wrong with my harness, or my feet.

Don't draw the straps too tight, give me freedom to move my head. If you insist on me wearing blinkers to keep me from looking round, at least see to it that they do not press against my eyes.

Don't make my load too heavy, and don't leave me tied up in the rain. Have me well shod.

Examine my teeth when I do not eat; I may have an ulcerated tooth, and that you know, is very painful. Do not tie my head in an unnatural position, or take away my best defence against flies and mosquitoes by cutting off my tail.

I cannot tell you when I'm thirsty, so please give me pure cold water frequently. Do all you can to protect me from the sun, and throw a cover over me, not when I'm working, but when I'm standing out in the cold. Don't force an ice cold bit into my mouth, but warm it first in some warm water, or in your hand.

I always try to do cheerfully the work you require of me, and day and night I stand for hours waiting for you.

And finally, Oh My Master, when my useful strength is gone, do not turn me out to starve or freeze, nor sell me to some cruel owner to be slowly tortured and starved to death, but do Thou My Master, take my life in the kindest way, and your God will reward you here and hereafter. You may not think me irreverent if I ask this in the name of Him who was born in a stable. *AMEN.*

*(Author unknown)*

# DIALECT OF THE SKELDYKE
## 1920's and 30's

The dialect was very distinct in this era and we learned it from our parents, grandparents and, perhaps most of all, from the farm workers who were typical Fenlanders. However, only once in my career in the Royal Air Force Regiment during World War II did anyone guess correctly where I was born in the British Isles. Strange as it may seem, it was a Welshman who had married a Boston girl.

The Ashwell family who lived close by had a very strong dialect, originating as they did from the Midville Fen area. This is no disrespect for that area that lies between Boston and Spilsby, almost at the foot of the Lincolnshire Wolds. The family is mentioned in the Skeldyke story.

My father had some strange sayings such as, 'You can't make good wool out of arse locks'. Meaning the wool from the backside of a sheep was no use for anything, therefore he could not do a good job with the very poor material he was working with.

If we were found doing something wrong as children, he would say, 'I'm not going to run after you, I'll catch you when you come home to bed'. This remark was more severe than his punishment because he would have cooled down by the time we arrived home. But I have to say that both he and mother were respected and loved, even if we did get a clip round the ears for doing wrong that did us no harm, but installed a sense of discipline.

Perhaps it was the same as children that I found to be the case in the RAF, there was only one crime, getting caught!

'You'll never get owt for nowt', meaning nothing is free, is as true today as it was some seventy or more years ago.

Horses understood simple commands and father had a canny way with them driving a team of three with only one rein or line as it was known, attached to the middle horse. A simple 'Go On', or clicking of the teeth would get them moving, and they stopped immediately on the command of 'Whoa'. 'Gee-up' was turning right and on the command of 'Cubbea' they turned left.

It is interesting to note that in what was called 'the olden days', when wagoner, garthmen, shepherd and labourer were hired by the year, they were known as 'confined men'.

This is a list of dialect that I was familiar with in the 1920's and 30's, but there may be more that I have forgotten!

**ARSE-END-UP**:  This was a real farm expression meaning upside down. 'He slithered in the dake arse-end-up'.

**BASS**:  Nothing to do with fish but was a lunch bag made of straw like material used by many farm workers, including my father and grandfather.

**BO'D**:  Bird. 'The bo'ds are singing'.

**BACKEND**:  Referring to the Autumn being at the back end of the year.

**BO'N**:  Burn. 'Bo'n that rubbish before you leave the field'.

**BREED**:  Breadth or width. 'Take a breed', father would say, that was confusing at first.  But it was always a breed with harrows, cultivating drag and corn drill, plus other variations.

**BING**:  A large rat proof box. 'Dad kept his corn in a bing'.

**BEASTLINGS**:  Sounds like beslins, it is the first milk drawn from a cow after the birth of a calf.  It is rich in protein and delicious, we enjoyed drinking it straight from the bucket.

**BOTTLE**:  Not as in bottle of milk, but refers to a bundle of straw or hay. 'Fetch a bottle of straw for the pigs'.

**CADYARD**:  Sometimes referred to as a Caddy Yard.  A place where dead animals are taken for disposal.

**CHELP**:  Insulting, arrogant. 'Less o' your chelp or I'll ding you round the ears'.

**CHEPS**:  Refers to the face around the lips. 'Wipe your cheps'.

**CHITTERING**: Talking. 'Chittering like birds'. It was an expression usually used by the men because - dare I say it - it referred to a group of women.

**CINDERS**: Ashes from a coal fire that were used to re-surface paths. 'Ours was a cinder pad'.

**COB**: On a farm, a cob can mean a number of things. It is the centre of a fruit, the centre of an ear of maize, a male swan, a short-legged horse and a round loaf of bread. A cob was also a small round stack that was the remains of a field of corn that could not be accommodated in one big stack.

**CODGERS**: Gooseberries.

**CRAWS:** Crows.

**CACK-HANDED**: Left-handed. Perhaps I am partly in this group. I hold a sweeping brush and all garden tools with my left-hand at the bottom of the shaft, right-hand at the top, the tool is on the right of my body. If I were to play cricket, which I don't, I would also hold the bat with my left-hand at the bottom and right-hand at the top. The bat would therefore be on the left of my body. Interesting, is it not?

**DACKER-DOWN**: This means to slow down, often refers to wind slowing down from gale force. 'The wind should soon dacker-down'. It also refers to speed, walking or running for example. 'Dacker-down a bit, I can't keep up wi' yer'.

**DAKE**: Meaning dyke or ditch.

**DING**: A word used by father. 'If you don't behave you'll get a ding round the ears'. This meant he would hit us with his hand.

**DINT**: Dent. Meaning to dent something. 'You'll dint that bucket if you don't stop banging it on that iron tub'.

**DOSSENT**: Meaning dare not.

**DYLINGS**: The best way to describe them is as ridges and hollows, the hollows being about nine or ten yards apart. They are designed for drainage, I only saw them in grass fields but can be used on arable land.

**ESH**: Refers to ash trees.

**FAGS:** Not the cigarette type, of course, but are lice found in the wool of sheep.

**FATHOM**: Nothing to do with depth of water but to understand something. 'I can't fathom it out'. Meaning I don't understand it.

**FEN NIGHTINGALES**: They are croaking frogs. I doubt if there are any in the Skeldyke area today, but maybe found in the Marsh area.

**FORE-ELDERS:** Forefathers.

**FOSDYKE LABOURERS:** They are seagulls. When they are returning home at night from the Skeldyke area they always seemed to be heading for Fosdyke on the edge of the Wash. Hence the reason for the name.

**FUN:** This does not refer to enjoyment, but to have found something. 'I fun a penny'.

**GATRUM:** A short narrow road, or lane leading from one field to another, or from the road to a field.

**GAWPING:** Means staring at something. A boy not taking his eyes off a girl, for example. 'Don't stand there gawping, get on with your work'.

**GLEANING**: After the sheaves had been cleared from a corn field and all loose straw had been raked up, it was still possible to glean, pick-up, enough heads of corn to feed our chickens for months.

**GOB-SLOBBIN**: Kissing. This is what took place on the last bus home on a Saturday night!

**GRUN:** Ground. 'Corn was grun at the mill'.

**GRESS:** Grass.

**GIN:** 'Not for drinking'! Meaning near. The 'g' sounds the same as in gain. 'Tatie graves were gin a road'.

**HACK:** Using a knife that is not sharp. 'Don't hack it, get the knife sharpened'.

**HAGGLE:** Arguing over a price, in the market for example.

**HALES:** Refers to the handles on farm implements and a wheelbarrow. I was told on more than one occasion that there were two hales on a plough and I had two hands. 'Keep tight hold of both them hales'.

**HUGGER:** A leather holder fitted to the back of a trouser belt to carry a round rub-stone for sharpening tools, mainly a scythe.

**HUGGIN:** Carrying corn from a threshing drum was referred to as 'Huggin corn'.

**HOVERS:** Sounded like huvers. Grass, foliage and reeds grow to a length of some four or five feet in the dykes and each year were cut usually with a scythe. It was then laid on the dyke banks to dry that turned the colour from green to a dirty brown. It was then referred to as huvers and became valuable material. Huvers was placed on the top of 'tatie' graves and heaps of sugar beet, the latter while waiting to be transported to the factory, in both cases to keep off the frost. They were also used on the top of a cob of corn that could not be thatched.

**JASPERS:** Wasps

**KELTER:** Rubbish. 'Get rid of that kelter out of the shed'.

**LARNT:** Learn. 'He larnt now't at school'. (Including the author!!!)

**LESK:** Refers to the groin.

**LETHER:** Ladder as used on farms.

**LOST WI' MUCK:** Filthy. We were often described as 'lost wi' muck' after a day down the Marsh.

**MANTLE**: Nothing to do with lamps. It means to walk aimlessly up and down. 'Stop mantling about, you're getting on mi'nerves'.

**MASH**: Could be mashed potatoes, but refers to brewing tea. 'The kettles boiling, mash the tea'.

**NOWTER**: Means the person is no use to anyone. 'He's a nowter'. Could be a she of course.

**ODD**: Means solitary. 'There's an odd house between Blossom Hall and Ivy House'.

**ORTS**: Refers to food left on a dinner plate for example. 'If you don't eat up your orts you'll have them for your tea'.

**OURSENS**: Ourselves.

**'OSSES**: Horses.

**PAG**: Means to carry another person on your back. 'Your getting tired so I'll pag you all the way home'.

**RECH**: Could be associated with reach, but is a measured distance between two sticks, usually thack-pegs, for example. Rows of 'tates' one hundred yards long shared between ten people means that ten reches each ten yards long would be paced and marked by the pegs. Each person had ten yards of tates to pick in every row for the princely sum in the early 1930's of 4/- (20p) for a full day's work. I started with a half rech at ten years old, graduated to a three-quarter at twelve and a full rech at fourteen years of age.

**RECKLIN**: The smallest pig in a litter. Such a small pig could be bought very cheaply, then with tender care could produce some very good bacon.

**SHUFTI-DEKKO**: To take a quick look.

**SLAP**: To spill. When carrying water in buckets, usually to a steam-threshing engine, the instructions would be, 'Don't fill the buckets too full or you'll slap it all over'.

**SLITHER:** Slide. 'To slither down a dake'.

**SLOCKEN:** To put out a fire with water. 'Slocken that fire before you leave it'.

**SNECK:** A stable door was fastened with a sneck. Known also to be called a latch or hasp on shed and house doors.

**SPATTERIN:** Drops of rain, but not enough to take shelter.

**SQUAD:** Unadulterated mud. 'The ground is that wet that I'm squad up to mi' eyes'.

**STABBERS:** The rungs of a ladder (lether). Each ladder was known by its number of stabbers. The exception being the longest one of all that would reach the top of any stack and was referred to as a 'Thacking Lether' (Thatching Ladder).

**SUPPIN:** Drinking, often from a bottle.

**SWATHE:** The width of a stroke with a scythe when mowing, or could be termed a breed.

**SHANKS'S PONY:** Walking on one's own legs as the only means of transport available. This was the only means of transport used frequently by my paternal grandparents.

**SPUD:** This was another name for potato, besides 'tates'. 'We were spud picking on the marsh farm today'. It was also the name of a tool that had a small blade approximately 2" x 3" attached to a wooden shaft the length of a small rake. Its use was to dig-up thistles known in the farming fraternity as 'spudding thistles'.

**THRESHING TACKLE:** Refers to steam engine, drum, elevator and either a chaff cutter or hay baler.

**TACK:** Referred to not having very good food, or at least food that did not give enough strength to a manual worker, especially a farm worker. Large pieces of meat and plenty of vegetables were thought to be more substantial than just bread and jam.

**TAFFLED**: Ropes and string get taffled - tangled or entwined.

**TATES**: The correct name, of course, is potatoes. On the farm they are referred to as 'tates' and everything relating to them were known as tatie fields, tatie boxes, barrels and bags, seed tates, ware tates, pig tates and tatie graves.

**TEEM**: This is a strange word. In harvest time we had to teem a load. This means to empty a vehicle of its contents such as sheaves of corn, loose straw and hay.

**TEEMIN**: Or kelchin and silin, referring to heavy rain, for example. 'Its teemin down with rain'.

**TENT**: As a lad I had to tent pigs. This involved keeping pigs in an open field while they scavenged loose corn, other fields being out of bounds. A man with a gun would tent a field of greens to stop pigeons destroying the crop. Pigeon pie, of course, is very tasty!

**TUTS**: Refers to few personal belongings. 'Gather up your tuts and let's be off'.

**UNEPPIN**: A person who is awkward at doing a job.

**UPSKITTLE**: To knock something or someone over.

**WAD**: A three by two inch piece of wood six or seven feet in length with a piece of white paper fastened on the top ten to twelve inches. Two of them would be planted in line at measured distances at the far end of the field. The first furrow would be drawn keeping the two wads in line looking between two horses. On the return journey the furrow would be ploughed away from first. The two furrows would then be ploughed inwards to form a rig, or ridge.

**WAP**: A binder cutting corn pulled by three horses had six or seven waps on a spindle that flailed the corn towards the knives, the corn then dropping on a moving canvas.

**YERKS**: A piece of string, or leather strap, tied just below the knees to stop trouser bottoms trailing in the mud. The 'Old Timers' on the farm used this method, it was said it was also to prevent rats running up trouser legs. In the 1930's wellington boots became popular, so I had no reason to adopt this method.

**YOKE:** A wooden frame or crossbar designed to fit across one's shoulders to carry two buckets suspended on chains *(see photo)*.

**YUCK:** Not to express distaste, but to give something a sudden sharp pull such as towing a vehicle. 'When you move off don't yuck it'.

**YOKE and UN-YOKE:** The 'e' is silent and the 'o' is sounded as in box 'Yok and Un-Yok'. To fasten and unfasten horses to implements and farm vehicles. It is possible that yoke has been derived from the time when a wooden crossbar - YOKE - was fitted to a pair of oxen that pulled farm implements before the era of the horse.

# MY COUNTRYSIDE

Spring, summer, autumn, winter,
    Each a display of unforgettable episodes.
Marshes recycled to form magnificent landscapes,
    Sunrises and sunsets give days of splendour.

The farmer ploughing a deep furrow,
    With horses tight in the collar.
Seagulls hovering for food in their wake,
    From soil freshly opened to the elements.

Acres of corn, potatoes, and sugar beet,
    Grown on the rich fertile land of the Fen.
Dykes dividing the fields,
    Carrying surplus water to the sea.

Snowdrops and daffodils blooming on the road side,
    Swallows collecting material for their nests.
Sparrows chirping in the hedge row,
    Pheasants soaring on the wing.

Uncrowded roads, beckoning the cyclist and walker,
    To view this countryside of beauty.
Cattle and sheep grazing undisturbed in the meadows,
    Peace and tranquillity a joy to behold.

Soft breezes blowing in the trees,
    Rain falling gently on my face.
Snow on the ground heralding a white Christmas,
    This is my precious countryside.

© *Stanley Naylor*

'Leicester Square' with Blossom Hall in the background.
*Photo Stanley Naylor*

'Boat & Gun' Corner 1999, compare with 1932 photos.
*Photo Stanley Naylor*

A Morris motor car ploughing through flood waters at the
'Boat and Gun' Corner, 1932.
*Produced by kind permission of Norman Loveday*

Flood water at the 'Fleet Corner' 1932.
*Produced by kind permission of Norman Loveday*

Flood water at the 'Fleet Corner' 1932.
*Photo Jack Hall, Seadyke*

'Fleet Corner'. In the background, the school on the left, Sycamore House
is on the right almost hidden by old Wagon Hovel, all now demolished.
*Photo Stanley Naylor*

'Tin Huts' where author was born and lived for eighteen years.
*Photo Stanley Naylor*

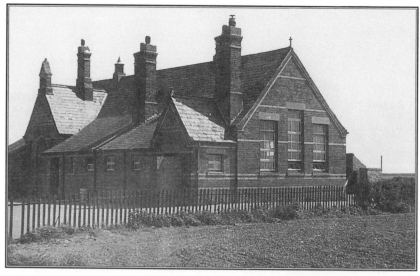

Kirton Marsh School demolished April 2000. Note the boys urinal with
no cover on the right of the picture at the end of the block of toilets.
*Photo Stanley Naylor*

1935 Jubilee.  Kirton Marsh School in Fancy Dress Competition
at Kirton, winning many prizes.

*Family Photo*

1935 Jubilee.  Fancy Dress Parade from Kirton Town Hall
to the sports field in Willington Road.

*Produced by kind permission of Boston Standard*

1935 Jubilee. Fancy Dress Parade from Kirton Town Hall
to the sports field in Willington Road.

*Produced by kind permission of Boston Standard*

Jane Bratley outside Burton House, Nidds Lane, in 1947 beside snow
piled high after being cleared manually with shovels.

*Photo Mrs. Bratley*

'The Nook'. Mud-and-stud house where author's wife was born.
*Family Photo*

A better view of 'The Nook'.
*Photo Keith Naylor*

Alice and Joseph Naylor, the author's grandparents. Photo taken in the grass field outside 'Field House' believed to be early 1930's.

*Family Photo*

Mr. W. H. Ashwell demonstrating the art of using a scythe.

*Produced by kind permission of Norman Loveday*

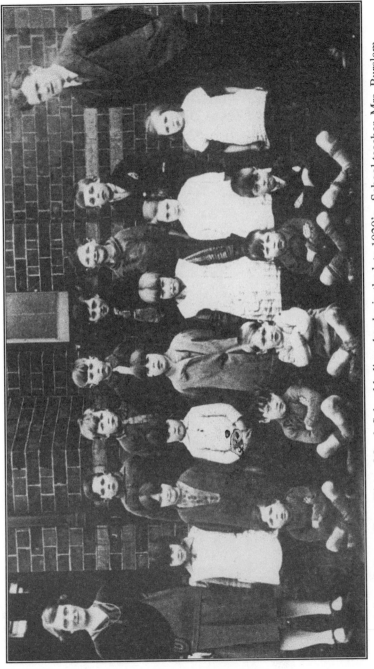

A few of the pupils at Kirton Marsh School believed to be in the late 1920's. School teacher, Mrs. Burslam, on the left and headmaster, Mr. A. Sentence on the right.

*Family Photo - Clifford Naylor*

95

Grandmother and Grandfather Naylor seated with the author kneeling aged about 7 or 8 years of age. They are surrounded by some of the large Naylor family.

*Family Photo - Clifford Naylor*

Grandfather Hezzell seated on the right with author aged about 2 years of age sitting on his knee. The only reason I am in the picture is because it was deemed to be unlucky for only 7 people to be in a wedding photo. The bride, Auntie Vi', sits next to Grandfather, new husband on her right, and Auntie Edith on his right. Back row: Uncle George on the left. Centre: Bridegrooms Mother and Grandmother Hezzell on the right.

*Family Photo - Clifford Naylor*

International tractor on iron wheels binding oats, August 1932.
Left to right in picture: Bertie Tunnard, Bill Hall, Jack Hall,
Violet Grooby and Earn Grooby.

*Original photo Jack Hall, Seadyke*

Fred Naylor demonstrating the use of a yoke. Note the familiar pipe,
watch chain, open waistcoat and rolled-up shirt sleeves.

*Family Photo*

A good example of a wringer used in the 1930's for
squeezing water from clothes on wash days.

*Picture Stanley Naylor*

Tools purchased by the author in the 1930's for
use on the farm and still in his tool shed today.

*Photo Stanley Naylor*

Tools purchased by the author in the 1930's for use on the farm and still in his tool shed today.

*Photo Stanley Naylor*

Flat iron normally used for ironing clothes, but similar to the one used in 1928/29 to strengthen the author's arms after his accidents.

*Photo Stanley Naylor*

Author aged sixteen working a team of three horses, namely Punch, Trimmer and Prince.  Note the tilted cap, open waistcoat and watch chain.

*Family Photo*

Fred Naylor, winner of a Ploughing Match in 1928.

*Family Photo*

Abb Dixon demonstrating his skills at a Ploughing Match.
*Photo kindly loaned by Ivy and Ray Dixon*

Fred Naylor with one of many foals he reared and trained.
*Family Photo*

Horse and cart, the cart fitted with raves ready for harvest work.
*Photo kindly loaned by Margaret Naylor*

Fred Naylor with four horses: Jolly, Turpin, Prince and Farmer.
*Family Photo*

Persons unknown, but the three horses are spinning out 'tates' for a gang of women pickers. Note weighing machine on the left. 1940's.
*Photo kindly loaned by Ivy and Ray Dixon*

Harvesting: binding corn at Cowbit Wash, 1932.
*Produced by kind permission of Lillian Ream Trust*

Typical harvest scene with Tom Samson and his team of three heavy horses, binding corn in the 1920's and 1930's.

*Produced by kind permission of Mr. F. Oliver, Show Secretary, Great Dorset Steam Fair*

Highly decorated horse harness worn for a ploughing match in 1956.
Typical of horses at ploughing matches in the 1920's and 30's.

*Produced by kind permission of Lillian Ream Trust*

Bringing in the harvest - West's Farm, Wisbech 1926.
Note the bonnet that was the normal headdress for women.

*Produced by kind permission of Lillian Ream Trust*

106

Agricultural show, Long Sutton 1945. Typical horse and cart combination.
Note the belly band to stop the cart tipping-up.

*Produced by kind permission of Lillian Ream Trust*

Watts blacksmith forge, Wisbech.
A normal working forge as seen in the Skeldyke.

*Produced by kind permission of Lillian Ream Trust*

Farriers at work, Wisbech 1933, as seen in the Skeldyke.
*Produced by kind permission of Lillian Ream Trust*

An example of brasses worn on the harness of
horses in the 1920's and 1930's.

*RAF Association Design,
Photo Stanley Naylor*

Cart or trap similar to the ones used by the Hall brothers and
the author's father to convey his brood to Quadring Fen.

*Photo Stanley Naylor*
*Produced by kind permission of Northcote Heavy Horse Centre*

Winding barrow for raising sacks of corn
shoulder high, to be hugged where required.

*Photo Stanley Naylor*
*The above photo and the following eight photos are produced*
*by kind permission of Mr. Julian Proctor, Long Sutton*

Two horse sugar beet plough.
*Photo Stanley Naylor*

Two/three horse plough, the depth determines how many horses.
*Photo Stanley Naylor*

One horse dual purpose 'tatie' ridger and hiller.

*Photo Stanley Naylor*

One horse skerry, used for cultivating between rows of 'tates'.

*Photo Stanley Naylor*

111

Two-horse 'tatie' plough, used when 'tates' were being graved.
*Photo Stanley Naylor*

Two-horse three row 'tatie' ridger.
*Photo Stanley Naylor*

One horse hay turner in the front. One horse rake at the back.
*Photo Stanley Naylor*

Two/three horse 'tatie' spinner. This type worked better in wet
conditions than the newer version with the 'dolly peg' and spider.
*Photo Stanley Naylor*

A gang (group) of women picking 'tates', spinner and horses
on the right, weighing machine on the left.

*Photo kindly loaned by Ivy and Ray Dixon*

Left to right - Ivy Dixon, Mrs. A. Reed, Mrs. D. Dixon, Mrs. Whittaker and
Mrs. F. Watson, pulling up mangolds for feeding cattle in the winter.

*Photo kindly loaned by Ivy and Ray Dixon*

A typical group of happy farm workers in the 1930's and 1940's era.
*Photo kindly loaned by Ivy and Ray Dixon*

Three men stacking what looks like mangold or mustard seed, but was a
typical stacking scene in harvest time in the 20's and 30's era.
*Photo kindly loaned by Ivy and Ray Dixon*

Corn stooks (stouks) near West Walton Church in 1950.
*Produced by kind permission of Lillian Ream Trust*

A typical stooking (stouking) scene in harvest time in the 1920's and 1930's.
Sheaves are being stood up to enable the corn to dry.

*Family Photo*

Abb Dixon carrying milk home from the farm. There were
no bottles left on our door-step before the Second World War.

*Photo kindly loaned by Ivy and Ray Dixon*

The illustration of the 'Gyrotiller' is an example of the machine the author
saw working at Kirton Marsh in the early 30's.

*Produced by kind permission of Robert Crawford of Frithville.*

Caterpillar tractor working in 1936.
*Picture by permission of the Boston Standard*

1923 Fowler Steam Roller.  Weight 12 ton.
Corner of living van seen on left of picture.

*Photo Stanley Naylor*
*Produced by kind permission of R. J. Heugh & Son, Boston*

118

The illustration of the threshing scene with the Marshall Eight Horse Power Portable Steam Engine, with the round corn stacks at the back, is the same as seen by the author in the early 30's.

*Produced by kind permission of Robert Crawford of Frithville*

1933 Type 6 Sentinel Steam Wagon.
Photo Cliff Naylor
Produced by kind permission of Tarmac Ltd.

120

Steam engine used for threshing with Mr. Smith at the controls.
*Photo kindly loaned by Mr. Horace Smith of Old Leake*

Full threshing set, steam engine, drum and elevator,
owned by Mr. Horace Smith.
*Photo kindly loaned by Mr. Horace Smith of Old Leake*

121

Typical threshing scene as seen so often in the 1930's.
*Photo kindly loaned by Mr. Horace Smith of Old Leake*

Threshing peas at Cockett's Farm, Terrington St. Clement, 1934.
*Produced by kind permission of Lillian Ream Trust*

122

Steam threshing, West's Farm, Wisbech, 1926.
*Produced by kind permission of Lillian Ream Trust*

Note the water bowser on the left of the engine and the hawser
wound round the turn-table under the engine. This is a different
view of the John Fowler engine as seen in the next picture.
*Photo Stanley Naylor*
*Produced by kind permission of Fred Coupland*

16hp John Fowler Steam Engine. Built in 1917.
Weight 19 tons when fully laden with coal and water.

*Photo Stanley Naylor*
*Produced by kind permission of Fred Coupland, Carrington*

'John', one of a pair of 18hp John Fowler ploughing engines built in 1925,
weighing around 19 tons when fully laden with coal and water.

*Photo Stanley Naylor*
*Produced by kind permission of Museum of Lincolnshire Life*

A rear view of 'John'. All four photographs of the steam engines were
taken at Carrington on 3rd October, 1999.

*Photo Stanley Naylor*
*Produced by kind permission of Museum of Lincolnshire Life*

This photograph was taken in Boston in February 1932. It shows the last
horsedrawn carriers cart that operated from Kirton to Boston via Kirton
Skeldyke that finally gave way to the motor coach. The owner,
Lawrence Richardson, sits at the helm driving Betsy and Daisy.

*Photo kindly loaned by Tom Richardson*

125

Lawrence Richardson, owner of 'Perseverance'.
*Photo kindly loaned by Tom Richardson*

A good example of a 1939 searchlight.
*Photo Stanley Naylor*
*Produced by kind permission of Mr. Houldershaw,*
*Allied Forces Military Museum, Stickford*

Two Bedford OB 29 seater coaches are good examples of those used by Cropleys in the 1930's, that eventually replaced the carrier's cart.

*Photo kindly loaned by Elsey's Coaches of Gosberton*

Author's deluxe Sunbeam cycle purchased August 1939,
ridden by his brother 'Bill', in the early 1940's.

*Family photo*

Chaff cutter, identical model as used by the author
in the late 1930's, driven by a static petrol engine.

*Photo Stanley Naylor*

# KIRTON MARSH

Two and a half miles from the village of Kirton is the Roman bank known locally as 'The Pullover' that has been retained as a second defence against flooding from the North Sea. Over this first sea defence there is a half-mile straight road that leads to the entrance to the main sea defence of Kirton Marsh built in the 1870's. Both Kirton Marsh and Kirton Skeldyke are part of the Kirton Wapentake that is identified in the Doomsday Book.

The new sea defence enclosed one thousand acres of rich arable land on the Kirton and Frampton Marshes that had taken a number of years to complete. For his valuable services in promoting the enclosure, Mr. Bett was presented with a very handsome *epergu, (a large silver or glass centre piece for a table).* On it was the inscription, 'Presented to William Bett, Esquire, of Fosdyke, by some of the land owners in Kirton in token of their appreciation of his great successful exertions in securing the enclosure of Kirton Marsh. April 1875'.

The presentation establishes the date of the enclosure, but there had been a dispute between the two parishes over the boundary involving a hundred acres. A costly court case at Lincoln ended in favour of Kirton, but a compromise was made where the disputed land was divided between the two parties.

Some sixty years on, I worked on the Kirton part of the enclosure and know this rich fertile soil produced some very heavy crops of potatoes and corn. Seeing the crops in recent years, it would appear that this rich soil is still producing abundance of food for the masses!

Climbing to the top of this sea defence that is locally referred to as the sea bank, gives the first glimpse of this huge expanse of the Wash. This vast area is in fact one of two of the largest estuarine flats in Britain, it covers no less than 250 square miles or 156,230 acres. The only other area of comparable size is Morecambe Bay in Lancashire on the West Coast.

The following figures have been gleaned from charts of the Wash that involves more of the Norfolk coast than I envisaged going as far as Blakeney Point. The distance therefore from the shorelines of Blakeney

Point in Norfolk and Gibraltar Point in Lincolnshire is 26.4 miles. The distance between the shorelines of the two counties from Holme-on-the-Sea and Gibraltar Point, this is the entrance to the Wash from the North Sea, is 12.43 miles. One of the widest points between the two counties is 17 miles from the mouth of the river Witham and the shore line at Dersingham. These valuable estuarine flats stretch 20 miles inland from Gibraltar Point to the estuary of the River Welland, the river that divides Kirton and Holbeach Marshes.

Four tidal rivers, the Witham, Welland, Nene and Great Ouse, flow into the Wash. These four rivers play an important role in the communities as they meander through the countryside of Lincolnshire and Norfolk. Over the centuries the silt they carry has built up the fertile soil of the Fenland's and the extensive estuarine flats of the Wash. The low-lying Fenland's are drained by a complex system of dykes and pumps, which feeds the surplus water into the rivers that eventually discharge into the Wash and the North Sea.

Each river is navigable in the lower reaches and is used by fishing boats to gain access to the fishing grounds in the Wash. Pleasure craft also use them to explore the Wash area and gain access to the North Sea. Cargo vessels entering the Wash use the rivers to reach the large ports of Boston, King's Lynn and Wisbech, and the small ports of Fosdyke and Sutton Bridge.

Leaving the Welland Outfall there are strange sounding names including Herring Hill, Clay Hole, Black Buoy Sand, Mare Tail, North Sand, Hook Hill, Toft, Roger and Long Sands leading into the Boston and Lynn Deeps. Lynn is half the name of King's Lynn.

The Wash is of very special wildlife value having international recognition for its contribution to the support of world populations of many wildfowl and wading bird species. The salt marshes have a high botanical interest and provide feeding and breeding grounds for thousands of birds. Large flocks of Brent geese visit the area in the winter and there can often be seen a small flock of pink-footed geese. Flocks of shelduck, mallard, widgeon and teal are the prey of the wild fowler. The Flats, as they are known, carry the largest wintering population of waders in Britain, they include knot, curlew, redshank, godwit, stint, snipe, dunlin, plover and shoveler. Flocks of linnets and twites may be seen, and there is one of the largest colonies of black-headed gull in Britain. In the winter months there can often be heard the expressive cries of the wading birds and the gag-gag-gagging of the geese across the mud flats.

Geese are very intelligent birds following a particular system when flying. They fly together in a 'V' formation with the bird in front creating an uplift for the birds following behind, this enables them to fly further than if they were alone. When the lead goose gets tired it falls back in the formation and is replaced by another bird. Birds at the rear of the formation honk to encourage birds at the front to keep on flying.

Seals populate the sandbanks around the mouth of each of the rivers Welland, Nene and Great Ouse, but are rarely seen on Kirton Marsh. However, during the flood tide one morning in September 1997, a young seal paid Kirton Marsh a visit and came close to the entrance. It did not like what it saw on top of the bank, a group of the human species, and swam on in the man made creek in the direction of Fosdyke. It would easily find its way safely back to the sandbanks with the receding tide.

There are small groups of the grey seal species, but the Wash is the main breeding ground for the common seal. Natureland at Skegness is worth a visit, especially for the children where seals can be seen in comfort.

To witness a flood tide is remarkable. I marvel at Mother Nature taking command of the Marsh covering it with water and not a blade of grass in sight. The only visible objects today on a flood tide are the tops of the two rails of an iron bridge that spans the 'Big Creek'. The depth of water in the creek when the tide reaches these rails is over ten feet, and the depth on the bank of the creek at that point is around three to four feet.

Viewing the Marsh from the top of the sea bank at low tide does not look at all inviting or picturesque, as the sea is many miles away to the left. The man made creek at the foot of the sea bank does nothing to enhance the view, it makes the foreground look more desolate. However, there is a natural beauty with the brown muddy creeks weaving a pattern amongst the marine herbage. But what is seen is not a tranquil wilderness, the long rough grass hides dangers that can easily drop a

131

person into a deep creek. The sides of these creeks are made of very soft black mud that can suck a person in up to the knees in seconds. It is good advice therefore not to be on the Marsh alone.

This incident experienced by my brother 'Bill' illustrates vividly what can happen to those who are familiar with the Marsh. 'Bill' enjoyed the challenge of the rough terrain in search of a dinner, that being his object and no doubt the reason for often getting a pheasant in his sights, perhaps not always on the Marsh!

However, 'Bill' and a pal, both experienced wild fowlers and conversant with the Marsh, were in their respective shooting positions when 'Bill' heard a cry for help from his pal. Investigation astounded 'Bill' who found his pal sinking in the quick sands. The only way the unfortunate victim could be extricated from his sinking position, was to pull him out of his thigh boots, which proved not an easy task, but was successful leaving the boots to be swallowed up in the mire.

This proves that the Marsh can trap the professional, but a good knowledge of the terrain helped in the above situation. Also tide tables need to be studied that are printed in the Boston Standard every week. The saying that 'Time and tide waits for no man', is absolutely true. Time just keeps ticking away and once the tide starts rising in the creeks there is no stopping the flow. As two men found to their horror when they were stranded at the 'Big Creek' corner, that I witnessed on a flood tide in September 1997. Fortunately they stood perfectly still waiting for the tide to recede, then I understand they walked off safely some three hours later. Hence the reason tide tables are important and need to be studied before venturing on the Marsh.

The creeks twist and turn all over the Marsh so the quickest way off is not always in a straight line, the creeks need to be followed to make a safe exit. Sheep and cattle tracks are a good guide, although I must say the heavy beasts do not make walking very easy.

As teenagers Kirton Marsh was our domain and playground during our spare time in the summer months. There was a corridor about a mile wide and almost a mile down to the River Welland that we knew like the back of our hands! When the Marsh was dry and using the plank that spanned the creek beside Mr. H. Tunnard's caravan and using a well-worn sheep track, we could easily cycle almost to the river. This is perhaps unbelievable looking at the Marsh today, but absolutely true.

We made our own entertainment camping, swimming, pulling samphire in season and catching a flat fish known as Buts. My wife's father would string a net across a large creek before the incoming tide, then after the tide had receded it was time to see how many fish were trapped by the net. The way to catch the fish was to walk bare foot in the water, tread on them, pick them up and throw them on the bank. I can remember timidly treading on that first large fish!

I was never very keen of swimming in the River Welland, although I always joined in. The current was usually very strong and it was difficult getting in and out owing to the brushwood on the sides of the bank.

Many enjoyable weekends were spent camping on the Marsh. When the tides were low tents was pitched on a patch of grass at the foot of the sea bank that was kept well trimmed by the sheep. When high tides were eminent then we had to pitch the tents on the slope of the sea bank. This proved precarious as I often woke up to find my feet protruding through the flap. Then on one occasion we were invaded by unwanted guests, one of the tents had been pitched on an ant's nest.

August Bank Holiday gave us the opportunity to be down the Marsh from Friday night to Monday night. The Monday was often referred to as the 'Annual Mud Lark', when some 1,000/1,200 people would descent on the Marsh arriving on cycles, motor cycles and horse and trolley, cars were few and far between. The local charity committee would have skittles, bowling for a pig, bean board and quoits. A local Ind Coope hostelry would have a marquee that was popular with the male fraternity, but out of bounds for us. I wonder why? There were minerals, crisps and ice cream that we could indulge in, and there was also a fish and chip van. Most people brought the ingredients to make tea except water, local houses provided the necessary hot water for a small remuneration.

Flood tides left pools of water dotted about the Marsh in which many people enjoyed paddling. At the same time they would collect the Marsh delicacy that was ready for harvesting at that time of the year, namely samphire, that can be cooked as a vegetable or pickled.

An early morning tide would give us our first swim, then down the river in the afternoon and at the evening tide every one gathered at the 'Big Creek' corner. This was the time to show family and friends who may only visit the Marsh once a year, how good we were, perhaps we tended to 'show off' in diving through an old car tube in fast flowing water and seeing how long we could stay under water. We did have, however, strict unwritten safety rules. We were always in a group that included some strong swimmers, which I never claimed to be, the strong ones kept an eye on the weaker ones and we never swam in an out going tide.

Safety rules on the marshes need to be strictly adhered to at all times. Never take Mother Nature for granted as she can be very cruel causing a lot of misery as the gist of this 1902 story portrays, that appeared in the local paper at that time.

'A day in the marshes at Kirton Skeldyke, near Boston, turned to tragedy on August 25th. A party of 7/8 people from nearby Kirton Holme went into the marshes for a family day out. Two of the ladies went for a swim in one of the many large creeks and were joined later by two of the men. The men got into difficulty in swimming out to the ladies who were in deep water, subsequently all four were drowned.'

This story is told as a timely reminder to treat the marshes with respect because of hidden danger.

During the summer months the sea banks around the Wash attract walkers, naturalists and artists who derive a lot of enjoyment from their particular hobby. As far as I am aware, I don't think that swimming is as popular on Kirton Marsh today as it was before World War II. This was a hobby that gave us a lot of enjoyment, it was a healthy exercise and it was free.

The Marsh was a hive of activity during the winter months and probably still is today, providing sport for those who liked shooting wildfowl. This sport, like a lot more, has never been of interest to me. but I have been associated with it through the brother already mentioned and father-in-law who loved nothing better than a few hours stalking these wild fowl wrapped in woollies and wearing thigh boots. In those days it not only provided a useful sport but it also put essential food on the table. Duck is very tasty and a goose was real luxury.

There was also an uncle on the Naylor side at Holbeach Marsh who with his two sons, were conversant with that part of the Wash. An uncle in Vera's family lived at Wainfleet who almost treated that part of the Wash like a second home! With the Halls who fished in the deeps and were also wild fowler's, the two families covered a large part of the Wash in their fishing and shooting activities.

In the 1920's and 30's it was known for wild fowler's to travel many miles, and probably still do today, from as far away as Nottingham, Sheffield and other towns for a few hours of their sport. One of the most interesting personalities to visit Kirton Marsh in the 1930's was Sir Peter Scott, son of the famous Antarctic explorer, Captain Scott. His mother, Lady Scott, was better known as Lady Hilton Young the sculptor.

Sir Peter Scott was an expert on the ornithology of the marshes and both a writer and painter of distinction. He made his home for some years in one of the two lighthouses on the River Nene that flows into the Wash. The estuary was a great inspiration to him where he could watch his beloved ducks and geese at close quarters.

According to my wife, Vera, on his first visits to Kirton Marsh, Sir Peter was in the company of Dr. Pilcher, a well know surgeon at Boston Hospital who was a frequent visitor to her home. Dr. Pilcher was a keen wild fowler and enjoyed hours of shooting on the marshes in the company of Vera's father, George Hall. George was an expert wild fowler and knew every inch of Kirton Marsh. On later visits Sir Peter spent much of his time with George's father, Jack, and his brother 'Waples' Hall. Both brothers were professional fishermen and wild fowler's using a punt gun as had Sir Peter on occasions.

The Black Houses, home to the Hall brothers, were situated on the land-side of the sea wall very close to the Meridian Line. Access to the houses was on top of the sea wall and they were half a mile from a tarmac road. The cottages were typical of that era, no telephone, no electricity, lighting was by paraffin lamp and candles. Cooking was done on the usual black grate that had the oven on one side of the open fire and a water boiler on the other, the privy was outside with the usual bench seat and vault. There was no bathroom, but that problem was solved by nipping over the bank for a dip in the tide, providing the weather was the right temperature. The weekly wash took the same form that prevailed at that time, the dolly tub and peg, clothes boiled in the copper and put through the wringer, *(see photo)*, then pegged on the line. The only means of transport was the trusty bike and a pony and trap that transported all the fish and birds to Kirton Railway Station, returning with groceries from the village.

Vera's grandfather, Jack, had lost his wife and living with him was one of his two sons, Sam, who never married and worked for a local small farmer. Also living with them was one of Jack's brothers, Edward, known as 'Teddy', who never married and worked on the same farm as I did owned by Henry Tunnard. Living next door to Jack was another of his brothers, 'Waples' and his wife. 'Teddy' eventually left the farm and joined his brothers fishing and wild fowling assisted by some excellent dogs.

The 'Walmer Castle' was the boat the three brothers used for catching shrimps and cockles in the Wash. Having experienced a few trips 'down below', as it was called, I can say that on a nice summer day it was a marvellous experience and very enjoyable, but it must have been horrendous in foul weather. The shrimps were caught in a net and emptied onto a large tray where everything inedible such as seaweed, crabs and the odd jellyfish was thrown back into the sea. The shrimps were cooked on the boat and bagged ready for a London market. They also harvested samphire that was in great demand in the London markets.

In the winter it was wild fowling. Shooting ducks and geese with a twelve bore shot gun would not produce enough to supply their market so they used a punt gun. The punt is a flat-bottomed open boat with only one deck about sixteen to eighteen feet in length. The gun is muzzle loaded and mounted on the front of the boat with the gunner lying flat on his stomach behind it. The gunner propels the boat with his arms over the side using small paddles. The problem being to get close enough for just one shot that belches black smoke and echoes all over the estuary. The recoil drives the light boat backwards, but that one shot could kill sixty or seventy birds, though twenty/twenty five was considered to be a fair average. But often there were days when it was impossible to get even one shot, the birds don't come in and, as we all know the weather is not very helpful, we get many rainy days. Wild fowling with a punt gun must have been one of the hardest, coldest and possibly the wettest way to earn a living.

A good example of the punt and gun can be seen on display in Ayscoughfee Hall Museum in Spalding.

As a sideline Mrs. 'Waples' Hall plucked some of the bright feathers to make flies for anglers.

The Hall brothers were among the best in their chosen profession of wild fowling. It is understood there may have only been around a dozen such professionals in the whole of Britain at the outbreak of World War II. Although it is known there were punt gunners on both Cowbit and Whittlesey Washes, it is not known how many actually depended on the profession for a living. It was very much a dying profession and no wonder, having to face the severe winter weather did not lend itself to encourage the younger generation to enter the trade. I believe the Hall brothers were a rare breed of men, true Fenmen who took a pride in their hardy way of life. They enjoyed the challenge of beating the elements and outwitting some of the craftiest birds that fly.

Even though living conditions on the edge of Kirton Marsh were sparse in the 1920's and 30's, this vast Wash estuary offered the Hall family a living. It offered the wild fowler a sport they enjoyed and put food on the table. It gave us teenagers' hours of pleasure exploring the wild terrain and swimming in the murky waters in muddy creeks. All this given to us free by Mother Nature. Perhaps our parents did not think it was free as the salty fresh air created hearty appetites that needed to be satisfied, but it kept us fit and healthy.

I believe, therefore, that the Wash estuary, or at least the marshes around the Wash, should be freely available to everyone without any petty restrictions. The enjoyment we derived from free access to Kirton Marsh was part of our heritage and should still be available today and for future generations. Providing, of course, the laws of the land are adhered to.

# THE WILDFOWLER

The Wildfowlers living on the edge of the fen,
    Was a hardy and professional breed of men.
Shooting ducks and geese for a meagre living,
    Facing the elements that are never forgiving.

The sound of flighting birds heralds a dawn start,
    To outwit them the gunner has to be smart.
Ducks and geese are the craftiest birds that fly,
    One hint of a human and they take to the sky.

The birds are unhelpful gathering in a cluster,
    The punt gunner must have patience he can muster.
Flat on his face with all the strength he's got,
    He paddles silently to get near for one shot.

Punt gunning is the wettest, toughest and coldest,
    Performed by the men who tend to be the oldest.
It's a memorable day when he gets that one shot,
    And knows that forty or fifty birds are his lot.

© *Stanley Naylor*

The Marsh road crossing the Roman Bank and second sea defence,
known as 'The Pullover'.

*Photo Stanley Naylor*

Gate to the entrance to Kirton Marsh on the land side of the sea wall.

*Photo Stanley Naylor*

View of the Marsh from the top of the sea wall at the entrance.
Note the 'residents'?

*Photo Stanley Naylor*

Bridge over the 'Big Creek'. Three quarters of the rails
can be submerged on a flood tide.

*Photo Stanley Naylor*

Photo taken from the 'Big Creek' corner, with the Creek
heading out to the River Welland.

*Photo Stanley Naylor*

Another view of the 'Big Creek' on Kirton Marsh showing the receding tide,
steep soft muddy sides and undulating terrain.

*Photo Stanley Naylor*

141

Camping on Kirton Marsh, believed to be 1935/36. Left to right: Jack Hall jnr., 'Bill' Raymond Naylor, the author (note the braces, yuk!), the late 'Madge' Margaret Sentence, nee Loveday and Vera Naylor, nee Hall, author's wife.

*Family Photo*

Kirton Marsh.
An interesting onlooker! But note the small twisting creeks.

*Photo Stanley Naylor*

'Waples' Hall propelling boat to get in range of a flock of birds
to get one shot with the punt gun.

*Family Photo*

'Waples' Hall proudly showing one of his catch!

*Family Photo*

Three Hall brothers. Left to right: 'Teddy', Jack and 'Waples' with some of a day's fishing for shrimps and cockles.

*Family Photo*

Three men camouflaged for wild fowling in the snow. Note the huge catch using only double barrel 12 bore shot guns. Left to right: Doctor Pilcher, George Hall (the author's father-in-law) and George's brother-in-law, Wilf Dawson.

*Family Photo*

# CURRENCY, PRICES & WAGES

There were a greater number of coins in use in the 1920's and 30's than are in use today and they were as follows:

**FARTHING:** This was little used during that period but it was legal tender. There were 960 farthings to the pound and indicated as $\frac{1}{4}$d. in numerical terms.

**HALFPENNY:** The halfpenny was commonly known as the ha'penny of which there was 480 to the pound and indicated as $\frac{1}{2}$d.

**PENNY:** Commonly known as a 'copper' of which there were 240 to the pound, 12 in a shilling and indicated as 1d.

The farthing, halfpenny and the penny were all made from bronze, a mixture of copper and tin.

**THREEPENCE:** Referred to as the threpni' or 'thrupani bit' or a 'joey'. There was 80 to the pound and indicated as 3d. There were two different coins - the small 'lucky' round silver coin and the twelve sided bronze coin.

**SIXPENCE:** The sixpence was known as the 'tanner'. There were 40 to the pound and indicated as 6d. It was made of silver and was put in homemade Christmas puddings, which created some excitement at dinner on the 25th December each year.

**SHILLING:** The shilling was known as a bob' and was indicated as 1/- or 1s. It was made of silver and there were 20 to the pound.

**TWO SHILLINGS:** This was the 'two bob bit' that was officially the florin, but was rarely referred to by that name. It was indicated as 2/- or 2s. and was also made of silver, there were 10 to the pound.

**HALF-CROWN:** The half-crown was referred to as 'two and six', two shillings and six pence, or half-a-crown. This was the largest coin in use at the time and there were 8 to the pound. It was indicated as 2/6 or 2s. 6d.

**TEN SHILLINGS:** The ten shilling note was the lowest denomination of currency to be made from paper. There were 2 to the pound, referred to as 'ten bob' and written numerically as 10/- or 10s.

**POUND:** This was, and still is, the basic monetary unit of the UK, known as 'pound sterling'. It was also made from paper and indicated as £1 or £1. 0s. 0d.

**GUINEA:** This was twenty-one shillings, 21/-, 21s. or £1. 1s. 0d., it was neither coin or a note. The guinea coin ceased circulation before the 1920's, but was still used in pricing some goods. It is still used today in live stock market sales and there are two horse races held each year known as the 1,000 and 2,000 Guineas.

The following is a selection of prices paid in 1935 and can be compared to the wages paid to farm workers on a following page.

The Boston Guardian was the local weekly newspaper costing 2d., from which these prices, wages, advertisements and village news have been gleaned. The cost of posting a first class letter anywhere in the UK was 1d.

1 lb of strawberry jam . . . . . . . . . . . . . . . . 1s. 0d.
1 lb of plum jam . . . . . . . . . . . . . . . . . . . . 7½d.
1 lb margarine . . . . . . . . . . . . . . . . . . . . . 6d.
1 lb of best quality tea . . . . . . . . . . . . . . . . 2s. 0d.
Lean bacon per lb . . . . . . . . . . . . . . . . . . . 10½d.
Large jar of marmalade . . . . . . . . . . . . . . . 8½d.
Tin of soup . . . . . . . . . . . . . . . . . . . . . . . . 6d.
Shoes for women and men . . . . . . . . . . . . . from 4s. 11d. to 12s. 11d.
Made to measure suit . . . . . . . . . . . . . . . . . 30s. 0d. (£1. 10s.)
Ladies dresses . . . . . . . . . . . . . . . . . . . . . . from 14s. 0d.
Cinema seats . . . . . . . . . . . . . . . . . . . . . . . 1s. 9d. to 2s. 0d.
Bertram Mills Circus Seats . . . . . . . . . . . . 1s. 3d. to 7s. 6d.
Cigarettes . . . . . . . . . . . . . . . . . . . . . . . . . from 10d. to 1s. 0d.
1 lb Tin of Lemonade powder . . . . . . . . . . 6d.
12 pint bottles of Nut Brown Ale . . . . . . . . 6s. 0d.
12 pint bottles of Best Bitter . . . . . . . . . . . 7s. 0d.
12 pint bottles of Worthington Pale Ale . . . . 11s. 0d.
12 pint bottles of Guinness Extra Strong . . . 11s. 0d.
New Wireless (Radio) depending on make . £5
Car Road Tax . . . . . . . . . . . . . . . . . . . . . . £30
Car Tyres varied from . . . . . . . . . . . . . . . . 16s. 6d. to 34s. 6d.

A 12 horse power standard saloon car cost £205, the de-luxe model was £225.

A four ton drop-side lorry with a four cylinder engine was £325, and the six cylinder model was £335.

Henry Ford produced a two door basic car for £100 and it was advertised stating the buyer could have any colour for that price so long as it was black! This proved to be a rare piece of salesmanship.

The reader maybe thinking the prices quoted were extremely cheap, but they must be compared with the wages we were earning in the 1930's.

The pay rates for farm workers were controlled by the Agricultural Wages (Regulations) Act of 1924, so that on leaving school in 1936 it was known what my basic wage would be and that rises were automatic on each birthday, reaching full pay at the age of 21 years. I actually attained full pay at the age of eighteen years, then a year later in 1941, I volunteered to travel for King and Country!

The following table gives the basic rates of pay for male workers in 1935, more money could be earned by working after tea at an overtime rate, or at a piecework rate.

| Years of age | Per week |
|---|---|
| | s. d. |
| 14 and under 15 | 11. 00. |
| 15 and under 16 | 14. 00. |
| 16 and under 17 | 17. 03. |
| 17 and under 18 | 19. 11. |
| 18 and under 19 | 24. 00. |
| 19 and under 20 | 28. 00. |
| 20 and under 21 | 30. 04. |
| 21 and over | 34. 00. |

In today's money the starting pay of 11s. 00d. in 1935 equates to 55p and 34s. 00d. is £1.79. However, by the time I left school in 1936 the wages had been increased and my basic wage at fourteen years of age was 11s. 4d. and I think the full pay for the men had risen to 37s. Wagoners over 21 years of age received the basic pay plus 10s. 0d. (50p) extra to feed and look after horses that involved at least 22 hours more in the winter than the basic week of 48/50 hours worked by the ordinary farm labourer. Whereas garthmen received 6s. 0d. (30p) above the basic wage to feed cattle that only involved perhaps two hours on a Saturday afternoon and about four hours on a Sunday during the winter months. Less hours were worked feeding horses and cattle in the summer when they were in the grass fields.

Female workers over the age of 15 years received 6d. per hour. The working day was from 8 am to 4 pm with a half-hour break for lunch. A 7½ hour day therefore earned them 3s. 9d. and a five day week totalled 18s. 9d. Having just written the wages earned by girls of 15 and 16 years of age, it is realised there was discrimination between them and boys of the same age. While the girls were earning 6d. per hour, the boys, myself included, were barely getting 3d. per hour, which I'm sure today would cause a riot!

Seasonal work such as pulling peas was lucrative. If my memory serves me right, a bag of peas weighed 28lb., or two stone, which a worker got 9d. or a 1/- for filling. With a heavy crop of peas, a good worker would fill a bag every hour, it has been known for one person to fill four bags in three hours. Then there was the 'clever' worker who put a piece of brick or clod (lump) of muck (soil) in the bag, that was easily spotted by an eagle-eyed man on the weighing machine, the bag would not be so full, of course.

Potato picking, harvest time and lifting sugar beet would be done at piece work rates that enabled the workers to earn more money and the farmer to get the work completed in as short a space of time as possible.

The Agricultural Wages Regulations are very complex that I have condensed in order to give the reader an insight of wages earned in the mid 1930's.

# TRUE-BLUE-YELLOWBELLY

If you think that Lincolnshire's the greatest county,
  If you think South Humberside's not here to stay.
Then (excuse my dropping bricks whilst my metaphors I mix),
  You're a true-blue Yellowbelly all the way.

If you think our sugar beet is much the sweetest,
  If you think our 'tates' are more than passing fair.
If you think each pea and bean just the greatest ever seen,
  You're a true-blue Yellowbelly I declare.

If you follow Scunthorpe's fortunes every week-end,
  If you reckon Grimsby Town are sheer ballet.
If you'll starve to catch a glimpse of the Lincoln City 'Imps',
  You're a true-blue Yellowbelly come what may.

If you'd rather be in Boston than in Bali,
  Though the East Wind keeps a-blowing long and strong.
If you'd rather see the 'Stump' than a 'gyptians camel's hump,
  You're a true-blue Yellowbelly right or wrong.

If you think the road from Lincoln out to Skegness,
  Is more lovely than the road to Mandalay.
If you think our heaths and fens better far than Scotland's glens,
  You're a true-blue Yellowbelly I would say.

Should you reckon London's rather overcrowded,
  And prefer our country all round.
Where the roads are wide and free from the city to the sea,
  You're a true-blue Yellowbelly I'll be bound.

If you think our fish and chips are something special,
  If you think our air's the proper blend.
If you find our elderberry much superior to sherry,
  You're a true-blue Yellowbelly to the end.

If you think our Shire's the nearest thing to heaven,
  Where you'd like to spend your time exempt from care.
Though the way may not seem clear, never worry, never fear,
  Like all true-blue Yellowbellies, you'll be there.

# COUNTRYSIDE FOODS

Living in the country meant that most people had a large garden. Like many of them, ours was cultivated with horses and plough, as it was far too big to dig with a spade, father didn't have the time anyway. The soil, with the help of fertilisers, produced some good crops of potatoes and greens. Rhubarb and gooseberries were plentiful, and the next house we moved to had apple and plum trees.

Killing a pig each year provided huge amounts of meat. Sides of bacon and hams were hung from the ceiling in the pantry making it an easy job to cut pieces as required.

It has already been mentioned that country folk waste nothing and this applies to keeping and killing a pig. A pigsty would be at the bottom of the garden and the pig would be fed all edible waste, potato peelings, cabbage leaves and stale bread all went into the trough. When it was killed there were some very useful by-products. One of the favourites was pig's fry, this would be on the menu for a few days, plus some of it would be given to neighbours who would return a fry when they killed a pig. Mother would be busy making pork sausages, an odd pork pie and brawn, the latter made from boiling the head and feet. Nothing wasted!

The countryside provided various kinds of food that were there for the picking. Mushrooms picked soon after dawn covered in early morning dew fried with eggs from the chickens in the yard and bacon hanging from the ceiling made a good start to any day. As there are several varieties of mushrooms, it is vital that the correct identification is made between those that are edible and those that are inedible. Even I have to be very careful, as I am not conversant with all the species, my advice is to visit your local library who should be able to help.

There was always an abundance of blackberries around the grass fields that had hawthorn hedges. This black fruit made lovely pies and we would be eating blackberry and apple jam through the year.

Sloes need a frost or two to sweeten them to make a very good wine, so I was told. Crab apples were fairly safe from scrumping, they were too small and very sour for my taste, but understood the fruit makes a good wine.

The elder hedge is a natural resource, not just for bean sticks, wine and syrup, but a cordial, lotion and ointment can be made from the flower. There are no less than twenty-one recipes in the use of apples, fifteen in the use of blackberries, twelve using damsons, eleven using gooseberries, twelve using onions, sixteen using rhubarb, eleven using potatoes and finally twenty-four using tomatoes.

It was my intention to include a few recipes in this book that I knew were used in the Skeldyke during the years leading up to the Second World War that started in 1939. We all are aware, however, there are literally scores, possibly hundreds, of recipe books on the market and no doubt there are a few on your bookshelf. I am therefore going to give you the details of a book that must have over a thousand recipes that will be easy to make with simple ingredients, just like those my mother and grandmother used.

The book is titled 'THE ENGLISH COOKERY BOOK' by Lucie G. Nicoll. Faber and Faber Limited, 24 Russell Square, London, is the only address I have and there is no ISBN reference.

The book was first published in 1936, hence the recipes are relevant and the seventh impression was printed in February 1948. No doubt the book is out of print, but your local library might help in locating a copy.

Recipes are in categories of each of the four seasons, then towards the back there are 'The Ramblers Harvest' and 'Drinks For All Seasons', using many local ingredients.

Should you not locate the above book, then you may well find similar recipes in other books.

# THE LINCOLNSHIRE POACHER

When I was bound apprentice in famous Lincolnshire,
Full well I served my master for more than seven year,
Till I took up with poaching, as you will quickly hear,
Oh! 'tis my delight on a shiny night in the season of the year.

As me and my companions were setting of a snare,
'twas then we saw a gamekeeper - for him we did not care,
For we can wrestle and fight my boys, and jump o'er anywhere;
Oh! 'tis my delight on a shiny night in the season of the year.

As me and my companions are setting four or five,
On taking them up again,  we caught a hare alive;
We caught a hare alive my boys, and through the woods did steer;
Oh! 'tis my delight on a shiny night in the season of the year.

Success to every gentlemen that lives in Lincolnshire,
Success to every poacher that wants to sell a hare,
Bad luck to every gamekeeper that will not sell his deer;
Oh! 'tis my delight on a shiny night in the season of the year.

*Author Unknown*


It is understood the Lincolnshire Poacher was written in the eighteenth century, perhaps even earlier, who knows?  But it would be interesting to learn the name of the author and the reason for writing the song.

# TIT-BITS

## A POACHER'S EXCUSE

When charged with trespassing when in search of game, a notorious poacher confidently declared that he had only been hunting for primroses.

'Primroses' scoffed the prosecuting lawyer, 'Was your dog looking for primroses when the gamekeeper caught him with a live rabbit in his mouth?'

'No, he won't,' was the broad spoken prisoner's surly reply. 'That poor rabbit was lame, an't dorg had just nipped it up in a friendly way to carry it back to its warren when along came t'sour old gamekeeper an' started raisin Cain. It's a pity if one animal can't do another a good turn wi'out somebody making a crime of it!'

But this ingenious line of defence did not save him from a protracted stay in gaol.


## RULES OF THE INN 1796

NO  THIEVES,  FAKERS,  ROGUES  OR  TINKERS.
NO  SKULKERS,  LOAFERS  OR  FLEABITTEN  TRAMPS.
NO  SLAP  OR  TICKLE  O'  THE  WENCHES.
NO  BANGING  O'  TANKARDS  ON  THE  TABLE.
NO  DOGS  ALLOWED  IN  THE  KITCHEN.

FLINTLOCKS,  CUDGELS,  DAGGERS AND SWORDS
to be handed to the INNKEEPER  for safe keeping.

BED FOR THE NIGHT . . . . . . . . . . .ONE SHILLING.

STABLE FOR ONE HORSE . . . . . . . .FOUR PENCE.

## JUST RIGHT

| FARMER | Calling from the door of a country pub. (the Boat & Gun - perhaps) |
|---|---|
| | 'How did you like the bottle of sherry I gave you for Christmas Jack ?' |
| WORKER | 'It was just right, Boss.' |
| FARMER | 'What do you mean it was just right?' |
| WORKER | 'If it had been any better you wouldn't have given it to me, and if it had been any worse I couldn't have drunk it. So it was just right!' |

## THE MOON AND THE WEATHER

The following lines were written by Dr. Walsham How, Bishop of Wakefield, when staying at Bala. Unfortunately Bala does not monopolise the distinction.

The weather depends on the moon as a rule,
    And found that the saying is true,
For it rains at Bala when the moon's at full,
    And rains when the moon's at the new.

When the moon's at the quarter then down comes the rain,
    At the half it's no better, I ween;
When the moon's at threequarters it's at it again,
    And besides it rains mostly between.

## A DEFINITION

The squire visiting the village school, put a few questions to the children. 'And can anybody,' he asked, coming out with this poser, 'tell me what 'nothing' is?' 'Yes' replied one boy. 'It's what you gave me for holding your hoss the other day.'

156

## READY FOR HIM

A lady complained to her milkman about the quality of the milk he sold her.

'Well madam,' said the milkman, 'the cows don't get enough grass feed this time of the year. Why, those cows are just as sorry about it as I am. I often see them crying, regular crying, madam, because they feel as how their milk don't do them credit. Don't you believe it madam?' 'Oh, yes, I believe it,' responded his customer, 'but I wish in future you see they do not drop their tears into my can.'

## NOTICE IN A SCHOOL

THESE HOOKS ARE FOR <u>TEACHERS</u> ONLY.

Underneath was added:

THEY MAY ALSO BE USED FOR HATS AND COATS.

## COULD BE IDENTIFIED

'Where's your dad, sonny?'
'Down among the hogs.'
'Suppose I can find him'
'Yep. Guess so. He's got a hat on.'

## HEN WAS SURPRISED

'A most wonderful phenomenon occurred believed to have been in 1907. A poultry keeper placed a hen on fifteen double-yoked eggs, and twenty nine chickens were the result. It was said that the hen's bewilderment at this extraordinary brood from such an ordinary number of eggs was very pronounced. The chickens, which are black Minoreas, are now about three weeks old, healthy and peckish, and have been viewed by scores of incredible curiosity hunters.'

## OMENS, BELIEFS AND PRACTICES

Call them what you will but they were, and possibly still are, part and parcel of the countryside, Kirton Skeldyke being no exception. These are just an example as remembered from the 1930's.

A number of magpies together would bring this rhyme to mind:

> One for sorrow
> Two for mirth
> Three for a wedding
> Four for a birth.

When my grandmother dropped her glove she would say it would be a disappointment for her if she picked it up but if someone else picked it up for her she would have a surprise. Having picked it up for her on numerous occasions I never really knew if she had a surprise.

A knife dropped on the floor indicated a male visitor, a fork would be a lady visitor.

Being a practical person I believe the above is due to 'butter fingers,' defined by the dictionary as a clumsy or awkward person who drops things. Sorry Grandma!

Leaving the top off the teapot when mashing tea denotes a stranger calling at the house.

If your cheek burns someone is talking ill of you.

Should the palm of your hand become itchy it means you are going to be lucky with money and the saying goes 'rub it on wood and it is sure to come good.'

When getting married the bride should wear:

> Something old, something new,
> Something borrowed, something blue.

When seeing a new moon for the first time make a wish while turning over the money in your pocket.

I wonder why coal was thought to be lucky when found in ones Christmas stocking? Likewise when a piece of coal was found on the road it was said that if it was taken straight home and put on the fire it was sure to be lucky.

Make a wish when hearing the cuckoo for the first time, it would be sure to come true.

Associated with horses is the mandrake. There is also a female version. The mandrake grows in hedge bottoms and grows all over it like ivy. It was the root that father used to dig out each year. A couple would supply his needs. I never did know the recipe but he fed it to the horses in very minute quantities. Whether it was the mandrake or some other concoction he used I don't know but the coats used to shine like silk and they took a lot of handling.

Wasps are those insects that sport yellow and black jerseys and leave a sting that causes some pain. Should one land on your flesh don't try to kill it because when you hit it that is when it will dig its hind quarters into your skin. Instead try to flick it off with your fingers. The old remedy for wasps stings was the blue bag mother used on wash days.

Cow dung, or cow-pats, soaked in water makes good fertiliser for tomato plants and the tomatoes taste beautiful.

Pure horse manure was plentiful in the 1930's and was and still is a good fertiliser for rhubarb. I have to say that today a granular fertiliser is more convenient.


**WEATHER**

The following are a few weather predictions that were often correct. Coincidences? I don't know. You'll have to form your own opinion.

> A red sky at night, a shepherds delight.
> (a good sign that the following day will be sunny and dry)
>
> A red sky in the morning, a shepherds warning.
> (a sign of bad weather in the near future)

Rain before seven, fine by eleven (am).
(more than not, I have known this to happen, especially if it was an early morning tide)

The tide is said to have an effect on the weather. Rain will come in as the tide enters the Wash and the rain will follow the tide out to sea. Coincidence? Perhaps.

I know that when seagulls bunch together on the playing field behind our house bad weather is imminent.

If there is enough ice to bear a duck in November, the rest of the year will be slush and muck.

'February fill dyke, March muck it out.' Meaning that February is often a very wet month and March is dry with some of those icy cold east winds.


## CONVERSION TABLES

| | | |
|---|---|---|
| 16 drams . . . . . . . . . . . . . . | 1 ounce oz | |
| 16 ounces . . . . . . . . . . . . . | 1 pound . . . . . . . . . | lb |
| 14 pounds . . . . . . . . . . . . . | 1 stone . . . . . . . . . | st |
| 2 stones . . . . . . . . . . . . . . | 1 quarter . . . . . . . . | qtr |
| 4 quarters . . . . . . . . . . . . | 1 hundredweight . . | cwt |
| 112 pounds . . . . . . . . . . . | 1 hundredweight . . | cwt |
| 20 hundredweight . . . . . . . | 1 ton | |

1 ounce . . . . . . . . . . . . . . 28.35 gms
1 pound . . . . . . . . . . . . . . 0.45 kg
1 stone . . . . . . . . . . . . . . . 6.35 kg
1 hundredweight . . . . . . . . 50.8 kg
1 ton . . . . . . . . . . . . . . . . 1.016 tonne

1 gm . . . . . . . . . . . . . . . . 0.035 ounces
1 kg . . . . . . . . . . . . . . . . . 2.210 lb
1 tonne . . . . . . . . . . . . . . 0.980 ton

```
12 inches (ins) . . . . . . . . . . 1 foot
3 feet (ft) . . . . . . . . . . . . . . 1 yard
22 yards (yds) . . . . . . . . . 1 chain
10 chains . . . . . . . . . . . . . 1 furlong
8 furlongs . . . . . . . . . . . . 1 mile
1760 yards . . . . . . . . . . . . 1 mile

0.91 metres . . . . . . . . . . . 1 yard
2.54 cm . . . . . . . . . . . . . . 1 inch
1.00 metre . . . . . . . . . . . . 1.09 yards
1.00 km . . . . . . . . . . . . . . 0.62 mile

10 mm . . . . . . . . . . . . . . . 1 cm
10 cm . . . . . . . . . . . . . . . 1 dcm
10 dcm . . . . . . . . . . . . . . 1 m
1000 m . . . . . . . . . . . . . . 1 km

1 pint . . . . . . . . . . . . . . . . 0.568 litres
1 gallon . . . . . . . . . . . . . . 4.546 litres
```

# GOD'S CREATION

He gave each flower its perfume,
   Each little bird its gift of song.
The wild animals the right of freedom,
   And we humans to nurture them along.

He gave us the humble 'tater',
   And the corn to make our bread.
Water to quench our thirst, life's nectar'
   So many miracles, it has to be said.

Mother earth is a magnificent place,
   Full of joy, sounds and perpetual song.
Beautiful colours glowing from the sun's blaze,
   With the moon shining all night long.

The beauty of nature is all around,
   With butterflies and birds soaring in the air.
A carpet of flowers on the ground,
   And the sweet smell of hay in the meadow there.

God created the trees that waft in the breeze,
   Where the blackbird's song heralds rain.
Where the crow builds its nest high with ease,
   And the cuckoo sings all day long without shame.

We thank you dear God for this precious countryside,
   For all things great and small we treasure with pride.
For the colour, beauty and joy it all brings,
   For the pleasure of living with these wonderful things.

© *Stanley Naylor*

# SUNRISE - SUNSET

Dawn breaks after a tranquil night,
    The day emerges with the first streak of light.
See the sun's first gentle glow,
    As it rises over the horizon so low.

The dawn chorus heralds the start of the day,
    The rooster displays his plumage, ready to play.
The blackbird and thrush create a rhapsody,
    The skylark and dove join in harmony.

A carpet of grass glistens with morning dew,
    Flowers open their petals to another day new.
The sun shines bright as it reaches its pinnacle.
    Mother Nature rejoices in its daily miracle.

The day draws to an end, evening shadows close,
    Flowers expel their perfume, drooping in repose.
Birds return to their haven, animals to their lair,
    Man to his home, his solace is there.

The sun disappears over the edge of the world!
    The moon filters through as it's unfurled.
The countryside sleeps, it's a magnificent sight,
    As once more it's bathed in the stillness of night.

© *Stanley Naylor*

# GLOSSARY

**BUTS:**  This is a flat salt water fish found on Kirton Marsh.

**COPPER:**  In iron receptacle built in a brick surround heated by a coal fire.   Used mainly for boiling clothes on wash day, which was traditionally on a Monday.  It was used for boiling the water when killing a pig, and on the farm it was needed to cook pig tates.

**CREWYARD:**  Partly open to the elements, but mainly covered areas for housing cattle and horses during the winter months.

**COBBLER:**  A person who repairs boots and shoes, or mends them, as it is often referred.

**DUNNY:** An Australian name for an outside lavatory.

**DOLLY-TUB:**  Used to wash clothes by hand using a dolly-peg.

**DOLLY-PEG:**  A twenty-four/thirty inch 'T' shaped handle with a round piece at the bottom looking like a five legged stool that was used to revolve the clothes in the tub.  This was hard work for the women who had strong arms and tackled this weekly wash with vigour.

**FLEET CORNER:**  This corner was barely one hundred yards from where I lived and known locally by this name.

**GARTHMEN:**   A man who fed and nurtured cattle mainly in the winter months, they didn't require so much attention in the summer when in the grass fields.

**GRAVES or CLAMPS:**  The bulk of the late crop of tates would be stored in a heap at the end of the field, or close to a tarmac road, known by the farming fraternity as a grave.  The base would be seven to eight feet wide tapering to a point at the top like an inverted 'V' and could be a hundred yards or more in length.  Initially the crop would be covered by a thick layer of straw, then before winter two layers of soil would be added.  On the top would be a layer of huvers.

**HARROWS:**  A farm implement consisting of an iron frame three or four feet square with spikes or tines used to cultivate, break-up and level ploughed land.  Three would be used in a set.

**ICKING STICK:**  Lifting stick.  This was a stick about two feet in length made from a broken shaft of any hand tool.  The stick was used by two men to lift sacks of 'tates' onto a vehicle, one working right-handed and the other left-handed.  It was also the means of lifting sacks of 'tates' onto a man's shoulder.  Having carried hundreds of sacks in this manner, I was informed by a tailor many years later when being measured for a jacket, that my right shoulder was lower than the left.  Hence extra padding being used to offset the deformity.

**LEICESTER SQUARE:**  This is the name that I refer to the corner at the top of Skeldyke, as shown on the hand-drawn map.  I am aware that some locals called it 'Hyde Park Corner' and others knew it as 'Kirton Corner'.

**LONG-GEARS:**  Harness that was put on the two front horses in a team of three pulling a wagon, the third horse would be in the shafts.  Chains on the harness would be attached to hooks at the front of the shafts that had to be kept taught or the horse in the shafts got too much work.

**LOWSIN-TIME:**  The stipulated time for horses to finish work in the fields was 2.30 pm known as lowsin-time.  Except in harvest when they worked up to 4.00 pm they were watered and fed for an hour and then continued working until 8.00 pm.

**MANGOLD:**  A turnip type root vegetable grown to feed cattle in the winter.

**MANGLE:**  A laundry machine turned by hand to wring out water from clothes on wash day.  Often known as a wringer.

**MINERALS:**  Sparkling soft drinks including a favourite dandelion and burdock, also lemonade, orangeade, cherryade, coca-cola and many others.

**ONCE-GROWN:**  Tates that have been grown one year on the farm and seed saved from that crop for planting the next year.

Seed would not be saved from the second years crop.  Father always said that seed tates should travel south each year in order to move to different soils. Seed from this area moving to Cambridge or Norfolk areas, for example.

**PANTRY:** Often referred to as a dairy. A small room off a kitchen where food and crockery are stored.

**POE:** Also known as a GAZUNKA. An essential receptacle to have under the bed at night in the 1920's and 30's when the privy (toilet) was down the garden path.

**PLASH:** This applies to trees and bushes that have their branches cut half-way through and bent over entwining them in each other and held in place with stakes. This forms a very stout natural fence.

**PRIVY:** An outside lavatory with a wooden bench type seat and a vault.

**RIDDLE:** A round three/four inch deep wooden frame with various size wire mesh bottoms to separate tates. Ware tates needed to be a reasonable size and was governed by the mood of the markets.

**STEERING-HOLE:** When a corn stack reached the eaves, someone had to stand on the edge, a precarious position to say the least, to take the sheaves from the man in the cart and pass them up to the men building the stack. Making the 'hole' as safe as possible, was something akin to a bird building a nest, wheat straw was woven on the edge of the sheaves held in place with thack-pegs. Known on the farm as the 'Steering-hole' and not one of the best of jobs!

**STOOK:** Pronounced as 'Stouk' as in stout, it was always stouking and not stooking. Eight or ten sheaves of corn stood on the ends, or bottom of the sheaves, with the heads locked together form a stook. This enabled the corn to dry, as the kernel needed to be hard before being threshed or stored in a stack.

**SAMPHIRE:** 'Weed of the Wash'. This succulent marsh delicacy, love it or hate it, is harvested in July/August. It can be cooked as a vegetable when fresh, or preserved in vinegar.

**TATIE CHITTING BOXES:** Boxes, or trays, in which the tubers are spread to enable them to sprout strong healthy chits ready for planting.

**TYPE-STICK:** This was a blacksmith made iron device that secured the cart to the shafts and when operated enabled the cart to be tipped to shed its load.

**TYING SACKS WITHOUT USING A KNOT:** Frank Garwell, a work colleague in the 1930's, taught me this quick way of tying the neck of a sack of 'tates'. Place one end of a piece of string between the first and second finger of the left-hand, pass the string round the neck of the sack, under the left wrist and over the third finger. Make sure the string passes over the first loop held by the first two fingers and go round the neck again. This time pass the end under the loop over the third finger and pull both ends tight. No knot and easily undone, just take one end of the string and twist round the neck of the sack.

**WAGONER:** A man who feeds and looks after horses.

**WAG:** All Wagoners, including father, were affectionately known as 'Wag'.

**WHIST-DRIVE:** Whist is a game played by four players - two pairs - with a pack of fifty-two cards. Each pair attempts to win the most number of the available thirteen tricks. A Drive is an event organised to raise money for good causes. In the 1920's and 30's they where extremely popular, attendance would be well in excess of a hundred, even in the Skeldyke, and the Christmas Turkey Drives in Kirton Town Hall, would nearly double that number.

**WARE TATES:** In farming jargon, this was the top grade that went to the markets. Seed tates were medium size for planting the following year and pig tates were obviously for feeding pigs.

**YELLOWBELLY:** The origin of the name is not known, although I have heard varying theories. The poem by Victor Cavendish 'TRUE BLUE YELLOWBELLY', describes the Lincolnshire species admirably.

# VILLAGE NEWS 1934

## FEBRUARY

### KIRTON SKELDYKE

CHARITIES - A sub-committee of the Skeldyke Charities met in the Methodist Schoolroom on Tuesday evening, presided over by Mr. G. Thompson. The principal business of the evening was to elect a secretary for the forthcoming year, and, after some discussion, this office fell to Capt. C. Rolfe. A whist drive was also arranged.

CONCERT - An interesting concert was given in the Methodist Schoolroom on Wednesday evening by friends of the Anton's Gowt Methodist Church, in aid of trust funds. The room was well filled with an appreciative audience, who called for repeated encores. The programme included items by the party and individual items by Miss M. Calverely, Mrs. and Miss Taylor, Mr. Wilson and Miss O. Taylor. Two sketches were also given, entitled "Silence Under Difficulties" and "Doctor's Orders". Those taking part in the first being Mrs. R. Taylor, Misses D. Doughty, D. Pepper, L. Wilson and Mr. R. Jackson, and in the latter the characters were taken by Misses O. Taylor, P. Doughty, M. Calverely and Messrs. W. Sibley and J. Jackson. The chair was taken by the Rev. E. W. H. Ross of Boston, who thanked those who had helped in any way. A coffee supper was served afterwards by Mrs. F. Bucknall, who was assisted by many willing helpers.

## MARCH

### KIRTON SKELDYKE

HOME MISSIONS - On Friday a lantern lecture was given in the Methodist Schoolroom in aid of Home Missions by the Rev. E. H. W. Ross, who was assisted by Mr. J. Clayton of Fosdyke, who is the secretary for home missions for the Boston West-street Circuit. Following the missionary meeting a pleasing ceremony took place in the form of a presentation to Miss J. Wilson and Mr. C. Horton on the occasion of their coming marriage.

## APRIL

### KIRTON SKELDYKE

BIRTHDAY - Congratulations to Mrs. J. Naylor, who today (Friday) celebrates her 81st birthday. She still enjoys good health and activity. Mr. and Mrs. Naylor are very well known in Skeldyke, where they have lived for a great number of years. Mr. Naylor, all being well, will celebrate his 82nd birthday on Pag Rag Day.

## MAY

### KIRTON SKELDYKE

BIRTHDAY - Congratulations to Mr. Joe Naylor, who, on Monday last, celebrated his 82nd birthday. He is well respected in the district, and, considering his great age, enjoys fairly good health. Mr. Naylor has lived in Skeldyke nearly all his life.

## JULY

### KIRTON SKELDYKE

ACCIDENT - An accident befel Mr. Ed. Wilson, son of Mrs. and the late Mr. Wilson, of the Council Houses, Skeldyke, while potato spraying in the early hours of last Thursday morning. It appears that he caught his thumb in the chain of the sprayer and severed it at the first joint. Mr. Wilson was taken to the Boston Hospital, where it was found necessary to amputate the whole of his thumb. We understand that he is progressing as well as can be expected.

OUTING - On Saturday the members of the Methodist Church and Sunday School journeyed to Skegness by train, for their annual outing. The party spent a very enjoyable day at the popular resort, and had tea at the "Pavilion". The members and friends of the Mission Church also went to Skegness for their outing on the same day.

# VILLAGE NEWS 1934

## AUGUST

### KIRTON SKELDYKE

CHARITY SPORTS - The annual sports at Kirton Skeldyke, held in aid of the local charities on the Kirton Marsh on Monday, were rather poorly attended owing to the adverse conditions of the weather, which was showery and dull. The officers and sub-committee responsible for the organising of the various competitions were: Messers. G. Thompson (chairman), F. Naylor (vice-chairman), W. Loveday (secretary), F. Simpson (treasurer), A. Sentance, J. Holmes, F. Wilson, W. Fisher, J. Burton and C. Pope. The winners of the various competitions and those in charge were: Table skittles (in charge of Mr. F. Wilson and Mr. E. Simpson), 1. Mr. B. Loveday, 2. Mr. G. Thompson; bowling (Mr. F. Simpson and Mr. A. Dixon), 1. Mr. J. Bates, 2. Mr. B. Boothby; skittles (Messrs. W. Loveday, W. Hall, F. Naylor and H. Fisher), 1. Mr. G. Thompson, 2. Mr. H. Fisher. The spinning board was under the care of Mr. S. Pope and Mr. J. Burton. The attractions were few, no doubt owing to the bad weather, but, considering the result was satisfactory, and a creditable amount was raised for this most deserving cause.

## OCTOBER

### KIRTON SKELDYKE

HARVEST FESTIVAL - The Vicar of Kirton (the Rev. A. F. Collyer) conducted the harvest festival service, which was held at the Holy Cross Mission Church, on Sunday evening. The organist was Mr. A. Higgins. The church had been beautifully decorated and gave credit to the following ladies - Mesdames Rolfe, Harry, Tunnard, Holmes, Higgins, Jackson and the Misses G. Watson, V. Grooby and Dawson. The gifts were afterwards sent to the Sanatorium.

## DECEMBER

### KIRTON SKELDYKE

WHIST DRIVE - On Friday evening a successful whist drive, in aid of the Skeldyke Charities, was held in the Marsh School when 18 tables were occupied. The M.C. was Mr. A. Sentance, and the table stewards were: Messrs. F. Simpson, W. Loveday, J. Holmes, C. Pope and T. Jackson. Mrs. H. Tunnard presented the prizes to the following winners: Ladies - 1. Mrs. F. Killick; 2. Mr. J. Borrill (as lady); 3. Miss M. Toulson; consolation, Mrs. S. Taylor. Gentlemen - 1. Mr. W. E. Cox; 2. Mr. T. Mastin; 3. Mr. H. Dodes; consolation, Mr. W. Willerton. Following the whist drive a six hand partner drive was played, in which 64 players took part. The winners were Mr. L. Taylor and Miss R. Hall, the runners-up being Mr. H. Fisher and Miss M. Toulson. A competition for a set of calvers, which was under the charge of Mr. T. Jackson and Mr. C. Bemrose, was won by Miss R. Hall. During the evening light refreshments were served by a committee of ladies, consisting of Mesdames H. Tunnard, F. Naylor, W. Loveday, J. Johnson, G. Barnett, C. Garwell, G. Cooper, J. Parker and the Misses J. Dawson and J. Parker.

### KIRTON SKELDYKE

CHARITIES - A meeting of the Skeldyke Charities was held on Monday evening, when Mr. G. Thompson presided over Messrs. J. Loveday (secretary), F. Simpson (treasurer), J. Holmes, J. Burton, F. Naylor, H. Fisher, T. Patman, C. Patman, C. Pope, E. Simpson, A. Dickson, T. Jackson and W. Housam. Arrangements were made for the grants to the pensioners over 70 years of age and the balance sheet for the recent whist drive was presented and passed.

# VILLAGE NEWS 1935

## FEBRUARY

### KIRTON SKELDYKE

WHIST DRIVE - On Friday a whist drive in aid of Kirton Skeldyke Charities was held in the Marsh School, when 16 tables were occupied. The M.C. was Mr. A. E. Sentance and he was assisted by Messrs. J. Holmes and C. Pope as stewards. The prizes were presented by Mrs. Sentance to the following winners: Ladies - 1. Mrs. Gill; 2. Mrs. Watson; 3. Mrs. Penny; consolation, Mrs. Early. Gentlemen - 1. Mr. H. Dodes; 2. Mr. W. Green; 3. Mr. Roy Sentance; consolation, Mr. T. Mastin. After the whist drive, a six hand partner drive was played, when 60 players took part. The winners were - Mr. T. Bishop and Mr. A. Massingham, the runners-up being Mr. and Mrs. T. Mastin. The competition for coal was won by Mr. C. Patman. During the evening refreshments were served by: Mesdames H. Tunnard, F. Naylor, J. Barnett, C. Pope, A. Cooper, W. Loveday, J. Johnson, J. Parker, Miss Joan Parker and others.

## MARCH

### KIRTON SKELDYKE

IN HOSPITAL - We regret that on Sunday Mrs. H. Nix of Bucklegate, was conveyed to the Boston Isolation Hospital. It is hoped that Mrs. Nix will make a speedy recovery.

### KIRTON SKELDYKE

MAJORITY - Miss Fledda Stewart, of Kirton Bucklegate, on Monday, celebrated her coming of age. Miss Stewart will be the recipient of many well-wishes from her numerous friends.

## APRIL

### KIRTON SKELDYKE

JUMBLE SALE - On Friday evening a jumble sale was organised in the Methodist Schoolroom, in aid of Trust Funds, by Mrs. J. A. Tunnard and Mrs. F. Bucknall. Those assisting at the stalls were: Mrs. Pope, Mrs. Horton, Mrs. Blackburn, Mrs. Jessop, Mrs. Thompson, Miss. L. Robinson and Miss. N. Wilson. The stalls were soon cleared and the proceeds were satisfactory.

## JUNE

### KIRTON SKELDYKE

ANNIVERSARY - The anniversary services in connection with the Methodist Sunday School were conducted on Sunday afternoon and evening by Mr. J. Tunnard-Kitchen of Lincoln. There were good congregations present at both services and the children did credit to their trainers, Mr. T. C. Silson and Miss. Doris Bucknall, by rendering the various items in a very able manner. Mr. Tunnard-Kitchen gave a short address in the afternoon and the children taking individual items were: Rita Brown, Norah Barnett, Florence Howsam, Amelia Patman, Emma Howsam, Gwen Naylor, Joan Warren, Leslie Simpson, Norman Wilson, Harry Grundle and Raymond Naylor. In the evening the children again contributed an enjoyable programme of hymns, recitations and dialogues, and those taking part were: Frances Matthews, Audrey Curtis, Margaret Naylor, Sylvia Tebbs, Nellie Wilson, Emma Howsam, Josephine Warren, Joyce Russell, Dorothy Clark, Doreen Killick, Phyllis Watson, Sylvia Simpson, Bessie Bucknall, Maisie Hallam, Gwen Naylor, Alice Grundell, Margaret Watson, Edith Dawson, Bert Patman, Stanley Naylor, Jack Barnett, Peter Jessop, Roland Waton, Allan Dowse, Ronald Dixson and Raymond Dixson. Mr. Tunnard-Kitchen gave an interesting address, and the collections were in aid of the Sunday School Funds.

# VILLAGE NEWS 1935

## JULY

### KIRTON SKELDYKE

OPEN-AIR SERVICES - Last Sunday Capt. C. Rolfe, C.A., commenced a series of open-air services at Kirton Marsh. There was a fair attendance and the hymns were accompanied on the cornet by Mr. J. Patchett.

OUTING - On Saturday the members and friends of the Methodist Sunday School journeyed to Skegness for their annual summer outing. The party left the village in the morning and arrived home at night after having spent a very enjoyable day at the popular seaside resort.

## AUGUST

### KIRTON SKELDYKE

OBITUARY - The death took place on Tuesday week of Miss. Eliza Naylor, the third daughter of Mr. and Mrs. Joseph Naylor, of Field House, Kirton Bucklegate. The deceased who had only been ill for a short time died in the Leicester Royal Infirmary. The funeral took place on Saturday at the Gilcroes Cemetery, Leicester, when the chief mourners were: Mrs. Burton, Peterborough (sister), Mr. R. Forrest, Leicester (nephew), Mrs. Sharp, Horncastle (sister), Mr. and Mrs. W. Naylor, Holbeach (brother and sister-in-law), Mr. F. Naylor, Kirton (brother), Mrs. K. Ward, Leicester (cousin), Messrs. G. and R. Ward, Leicester. Wreaths were placed on the grave from: Mother and Father; Alice, Lou and Ralph; Nellie and Walter; Fred and Emma; Emma, Bob and Family; Will and Sarah; Minnie; K. Ward and Family; Eric and Winnie Ward; Mrs. Green and Family; Mrs. Ellwood; Len, Bert and Fred.

## OCTOBER

### KIRTON SKELDYKE

HARVEST FESTIVAL - On Sunday the annual harvest festival services were held at the Methodist Church, when the preacher, both afternoon and evening was Mr. W. M. Brewin, of Boston. The inclement weather had an adverse effect on the attendance at the afternoon service, but there was a fairly large congregation present in the evening, when Mr. Brewin preached. During the service a solo was contributed by Mrs. J. R. Morley, of Kirton, and the organist at both services was Miss. Doris Bucknall. The festival was continued on Thursday when a meeting was held addressed by the Rev. T. W. Brown, of Boston, Mr. J. H. Mountain, and others. After the meeting the fruit and flowers etc. were sold in aid of the Church Funds.

## NOVEMBER

### KIRTON SKELDYKE

WHIST DRIVE - On Friday a whist drive was held in the Marsh School in aid of the Kirton Skeldyke charities, when 19 tables were occupied. The M. C. was Mr. A. Sentance, of Kirton, and during the interval refreshments were served by the following ladies: Mesdames F. Naylor, H. Tunnard, Garwell, Johnson, Barnett, W. Loveday, Cooper, Parker, Thompson and the Misses N. Wilson, C. Loveday and J. Parker. The prizes were presented by Mrs. J. Holmes to the following players:   Ladies:- 1. Mrs. Bursnall, 2. Miss. R. Hall, 3. Mrs. Flower, consolation Miss. Brotherton: Gentlemen:- 1. Mr. A. E. Dixson, 2. Mr. B. Traves, 3. Mr. F. Barnett, consolation Mr. R. Bemrose. Following the main drive a six-hand partner drive was held the winners being Mrs. Pope and Mr. W. Grooby, and the runners up Mrs. Bursnall and Mr. G. Marshall. The cause will benefit considerably.

## DECEMBER

### KIRTON SKELDYKE

SHARE OUT - The annual share out of the 'Boat and Gun' Sick and Dividing club was held on Friday. Mr. T. Dawson (secretary) read the balance sheet which was considered satisfactory. In the men's section a dividend of 15s. 1½d. was declared to 115 members, and in the women's section 44 members received 9s. 8d. each. The officers elected for the ensuing year are: Chairman, Mr. W. Loveday; Vice-Chairman, Mr. E. Tebb;   Treasurer, Mrs. Kitching;    Secretary, Mr. T. Dawson; Committee, Messrs. J. Burton, G. Martin, R. Kime, E. Dixson, B. Martin and W. Howsam. A smoking concert followed when those contributing to the programme were:   H. Potter, P. Cannon, F. Naylor, W. Howsam, E. Dixon, W. Pitts, G. Bolton, W. Loveday and - Pitts.

# VILLAGE NEWS 1936

## KIRTON SKELDYKE

CHILDREN'S CONCERT - On Friday, the children attending the Methodist Sunday School gave a delightful entertainment in the school-room, when the Rev. T. W. Brown of Boston presided. There was a crowded attendance and the feature of the evening was a competition for the best given items, the judges of the competition being Miss G. Kibblewhite of Boston and Messrs. G. Wander and J. R. Morley of Kirton, who awarded the prizes as follows: 1. Emma Howsam; 2. Gwen Naylor and Joan Warren; 3. Amelia Patman; 4. Rita Brown. The children taking part in the choruses, action songs, duets, recitations etc., were: Amelia Patman, Brenda Warren, Masie Hallam, Alice Grundell, Bessie Bucknall, Nellie Wilson, Nora Barnett, Margaret Naylor, Audrey Curtis, Edith Howsam, Rita Brown, Gwen Naylor, Joan Warren, Florence Howsam, Emma Howsam, Raymond Naylor, Stanley Naylor, Peter Jessop, Jack Barnett and Bertie Patman. The sketch, entitled "Christmas Time", caused much amusement, those taking part being: Nellie Wilson, Amelia Patman, Doris Bucknall, Emma Howsam, Brenda Warren, Masie Hallam and Stanley Naylor. The concert was much enjoyed and credit must go to Mrs. F. Bucknall, who was responsible for the training of the children, and to the accompanist, Miss Doris Bucknall, who was assisted by Miss Nellie Wilson and Miss Bessie Bucknall. The Rev. T. W. Brown expressed his appreciation to Mrs. Bucknall and thanked the children and all those who had helped to make the event so successful. At the close, refreshments were served by Mrs. J. A. Tunnard, who was assisted by Mesdames Jessop, Simpson, Silson, Pope, Miss T. Tunnard and the children. The doorkeepers were Messrs. F. Bucknall and C. Pope and the proceeds were in aid of church funds.

## APRIL

### KIRTON SKELDYKE

BIRTHDAY - Congratulations to Mrs. J. Naylor, of Kirton Skeldyke, who on Tuesday celebrated her 83rd birthday. Mrs. Naylor enjoys good health, but feels rather severely the loss of her husband, who died some weeks ago.

## JUNE

### KIRTON SKELDYKE

ANNIVERSARY - On Sunday the annual Sunday School anniversary services in connection with the Methodist Church were held, conducted by Mr. J. H. Mountain of Boston, both afternoon and evening. The children taking part in the afternoon programme which consisted of hymns, recitations, etc., were: Audrey Curtis, Sylvia Simpson, Raymond Naylor, Florence Howsam, Bert Patman, Gwen Naylor, Emma Howsam, Bessie Bucknall, Josephine Warren, Dorothy Clark, Alice Grundell and Rita Brown. There was a large congregation present at the evening service when the children again gave a programme of solo's, hymns, recitations, etc. Those taking part were: Joan Warren, Leslie Simpson, Margaret Naylor, Maisie Hallam, Norman Wilson, Emma Howsam, Audrey Curtis, Raymond Naylor, Josephine Warren, Bert Patman, Raymond Dixson, Florence Howsam, Alice Grundell, Edith Howsam and Rita Brown. Miss Doris Bucknall presided at the piano and together with the teachers of the school is to be heartily congratulated on the high performance the children gave. Mr. Mountain gave a short address and expressed regret that the Supt., Mr. C. T. Silson, was unable to be present owing to indisposition, the collections were in aid of Sunday School Funds.

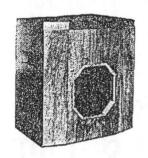 

# One penny provides a delicious Breakfast for 3 People ....

Every 7½d. packet of 'Farmer's Glory' Wheat Flakes is a BIG packet ... a 12 oz. packet ... a packet containing from 2 ozs. to 4 ozs. more than that of any other similar food at its price. This means a big wholesome cereal breakfast for 3 people for a penny! 'Farmer's Glory' Flakes are made of wheat grown in England ... flaked with malt made from English barley ... sweetened with English sugar ... prepared by English men and women ... financed with English capital. You are doing your fellow countrymen good by doing the *inner* man good with this delicious, healthful, *completely* satisfying food. Buy the best from your English neighbours — and save money every day of the week.

## *Ask your grocer for*
# 'FARMER'S GLORY'
## *Toasted Wheat Flakes*

7½ D
/2
EXTRA LARGE
12 oz. PACKET
8 oz. PKT. 6d

**THE WORLD'S FINEST BREAKFAST CEREAL**

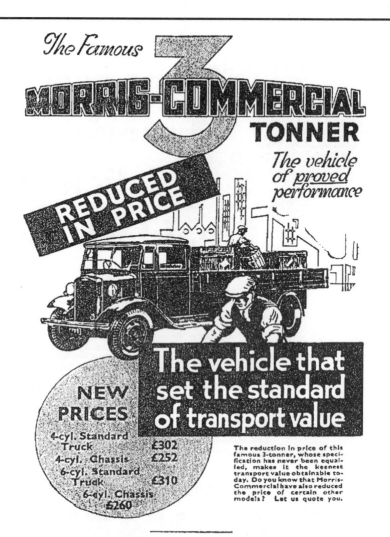

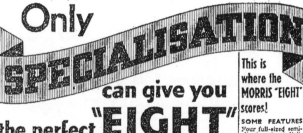

# Only SPECIALISATION

## can give you the perfect "EIGHT"

Here, at last, is an "Eight" that you'll get *real enjoyment* out of owning and driving. There's plenty of room in it—the body is as large as the average 10 h.p. car. There's plenty of "go" in it. It's built like a big car—it looks and behaves like a big car—yet it's so economical that it does 45 miles to the gallon. Come and let us show you what a great little car it is !

This is where the MORRIS "EIGHT" scores!

**SOME FEATURES**
Four full-sized semi-elliptic springs . . Full-sized dynamo with large capacity battery . . . Large 3-bearing crankshaft . . . Lockheed hydraulic brakes . . . Chromium-plated radiator. 45 miles per gallon and a speed of over 50 miles an hour. These are points that you can check for yourself by comparison. And you'll find many others,

In a wide range of attractive colours.

Prices from £118
Tax £8.
(1935 TAX £6).

## The new
# MORRIS "EIGHT"

E. C. STANWELL & SONS, WEST STREET, BOSTON;
F. C. JACKSON, CONINGSBY; TUNNARD & Co., KIRTON;
DAWSON & SONS, DONINGTON; C. A. SHARP,
SUTTERTON.

# HOLLAND
## - BROS - LTD -
MORRIS DISTRIBUTORS :

## Wide Bargate, BOSTON.

Phone 606-7.
2 Lines.

179

# New Theatre, Boston

TELEPHONE 135.

**MONDAY, JULY 30th AND DURING THE WEEK.**
Twice Nightly at 6.30 & 8.30.
Matinees Thursday & Saturday at 2.30.

JOAN CRAWFORD and CLARK GABLE in

# DANCING LADY,

Music — Dancing — Comedy — Romance.
Entertainment above the ordinary run.

---

# Scala Boston

TELEPHONE 135.

**MONDAY, JULY 30th AND DURING THE WEEK.**
Twice Nightly at 6.15 & 8.15.
Matinees Wednesday & Saturday at 2.15.

Monday, Tuesday & Wednesday.
CONSTANCE BENNETT with
GILBERT ROLAND in

## SEALED LIPS,

Also JOEL McCREA
in a delightfully human story—

## CHANCE AT HEAVEN.

Thursday, Friday & Saturday,
MADGE EVANS and OTTO KRUGER
in

## BEAUTY,

With ALICE BRADY and
UNA MERKEL.
A brilliant satire with genuinely amusing scenes. Beautifully acted and lavishly mounted.

181

# Shop at the
# International

## 'Sylvan Glen'

# BUTTER

### The World's Best Butter

### Is only 10$^{d}$ per lb.

*The Butter that Spreads*

Here is a notable example of International Value.
Sylvan Glen Butter, obtainable only at the
International Stores, cannot be surpassed for
Quality, Freshness, and Value.

## Shopping Is Most Economical
## at the International

182

*All adverts and village news are kindly produced by the Boston Standard*

183

# KIRTON-IN-HOLLAND

The fact that Kirton has a Town Brass Band formed in 1870, a Town Hall built in 1911 and a Town Football Club indicates it is a large village. It is surrounded by agriculture and horticulture industries, and in the village there are tractor firms, a tyre depot and vegetable processing factories all providing work for local people.

In the reign of Elizabeth I, Kirton was the third town of any size in the county of Lincolnshire. It was much larger then Boston and had only 231 less households than Lincoln.

The Doomsday Book refers to Kirton as 'Chircetune' indicating the village took it's name from the Church, which is not surprising as it stands so proudly in the centre of the village. It may well be that the Church of St. Peter and St. Paul stands on the age-old worship site of the Druids, and it is as impressive today as it must have been in its origins in the 13th Century. The building has survived various disasters over the years and today has some interesting features. They include a memorial window to the memory of a local lad, J. S. Paulson killed in the First World War, who's parents lived in the Sycamores on the opposite side of the road, now the 'Merry Monk'. The Lych Gate commemorates all who fell in that war, as also does the plaque inside the Church. There is also a scroll in appreciation of the work done by Dame Sarah Swift in the First World War who was born in Kirton Skeldyke. She was Matron in Chief of all Red Cross Hospitals and founder of the Royal College of Nursing. A unique feature in the church is the beautiful hand woven kneelers commemorating relatives, friends and Ex-Service Associations.

Standing proudly on The Green is the War Memorial reminding us of the eighty-four men who fell in the two World Wars, 1914 to 1918 and 1939 to 1945. 'LEST WE FORGET'. They include from the First World War, Sgt. H. Jackson VC; G. Smith DCM; T. W. Hardy MM; P. Feariss DCM and Bernard Cody, nephew of Colonel Cody, better known as 'Buffalo Bill'. From the Second World War there are the names of three lads who I knew from my school days, and even though I was involved in the conflict, it brings the reality of war close to home!

Also on the Green is Harvey House, a fine example of Georgian structure. Almost opposite the Church in Willington Road stands the old Grammar School established by Sir John Middlecott in 1624 and closed around 1917/19. The most notable pupil was Luke Hansard who went on to establish the Parliamentary Hansard Reports. The Secondary Modern School has taken the name of Middlecott and proudly upholds the fine tradition established by the old Grammar School. The new Primary School opened in 1975, has a comprehensive curriculum and is proud of its roots with the old Primary School that has just been demolished in King Street.

On the corner of High Street and King Street stands the 'King's Head', a 16th Century former ale-house that is now fully residential. One of its landlords was Johnny Cuthbert, the famous local boxer. Just along the High Street is the 'Peacock Inn', one of only three hostelries out of six that is licensed today, the other two are the 'Black Bull' and the 'Stag and Pheasant'.

Benefactors in the history of Kirton include Robert Hunt who bequeathed four 17th Century almshouses to the village. John Speak, who installed some of the stained glass windows in the Church and presented four more almshouses in 1928. He also provided the surround to the War Memorial, this is stated on the small plaque at the foot of the right-hand pillar to the gate near the bus stop. Sitting proudly on the forecourt of the Town Hall presented by him in 1911 is the statue of William Dennis. More recent times, the tyre firm of Fossitt and Thorne presented the Chairman's Chain of Office to the Parish Council on which I am honoured to have my name inscribed. The late Harry Thorne is one of only four residents who have been presented with the Kirton Village Award for valued services to the community and parish. The other three are the late Councillor Wally Franks and Don Flatters, and as Chairman of the Parish Council at the time I had the privilege of presenting the fourth award to the Rev. John Trinder in 1993. John had retired after being the Vicar at Kirton Church for a number of years and had also been involved with many organisations, one of them being Welfare Officer for the Kirton branch of The Royal British Legion.

This is only a brief account of the history of Kirton that is far reaching over centuries. Yet today it is a very busy village where I believe the only article that can't be purchased within its shops are a pair of shoes. A more detailed history can be found in the book titled KIRTON-in-HOLLAND available in Fossitt and Thorne's shop on the Green. The book is sold in aid of Church funds.

185

# BOSTON

Associated with the Wash is the market town of Boston. Sitting on the riverbank in the centre is the world famous Church of St. Botolph, affectionately known as 'Boston Stump'. The Church dates back to 1309, but part of it, including the tower, is of fifteenth century workmanship. Ancestors tell us this massive church with its tall tower was built on wool. They don't mean literally of course, but on the proceeds from the sale of wool, which was exported through the docks.

When you climb the Tower and someone says you can see New York, don't be surprised, it is a hamlet some seven miles away as the crow flies! On a clear day it is possible to see Lincoln Cathedral and there is an excellent view of the Wash. It is well worth the huffing and puffing climbing all those steps just to get a glimpse of these magnificent Fens.

The vital statistics of the 'Stump' are of great interest and are astounding to say the least. The height of the tower from the foot of the church to the top stone is 272 feet, 6 inches (approx. 85 metres). Aircrews have used the tower for navigation ever since flying began. It was a major land mark for bomber crews during World War II and is still used by the 'Battle of Britain Memorial Flight' based at RAF Coningsby.

The length of the church is 282 feet, 6 inches (approx. 86 metres), and 100 feet wide (approx. 31 metres), however, although statistics can be boring, the following appear to correspond to periods of time.

| | | |
|---|---|---|
| 365 steps to the top of the tower | - | days of the year. |
| 52 windows | - | weeks in the year. |
| 12 pillars | - | months in the year. |
| 7 doors | - | days in the week. |
| 24 steps to the library | - | hours in the day. |
| 60 steps to each side of the chancel | - | minutes in the hour and seconds in the minute. |

The River Witham is steeped in history including the first attempt of the Pilgrim Fathers to leave these shores in search of religious freedom. The Boston Borough Council erected a Memorial in 1957 at Scotia Creek at Fishtoft to mark the event.

Boston also boasts of having the tallest working Windmill in Great Britain, known as Maud Foster Windmill that dates back to 1819. Corn can be seen ground into flour and purchased from the shop.

Boston was smaller than Kirton when it was established as a Port, yet in the fourteenth century it was second only to London as the busiest port in the country. As the Port developed, so the town has grown to the size it is today. The Guildhall dates to 1450, the Queen Anne style Fydell House is 1700 and the Assembly Rooms are dated 1822. The Havenside Country Park is situated on a stretch of the River Witham that has a large wild life habitat and wetlands and is a good viewing point for ships entering and leaving the dock.

Famous people of the Boston area include Jean Ingelow, a poetess. Herbert Ingram, founded the London Illustrated News in 1842. John Cotton became the first minister of the Christian Church in Boston, USA. Sir Joseph Banks born 1743, a Botanist, sailed with Captain Cook in HM Bark Endeavour to the South Seas 1768 to 1771. It was largely due to Sir Joseph that New South Wales was founded and so he is regarded as one of the 'Fathers of Australia'. George Bass has his name immortalised in the Bass Straits between South Australia and Tasmania. Joseph Gilbert was an astronomer, sailed with Captain Cook on HMS Resolution and has the Gilbert Islands named after him.

More detailed information on Boston can be found in 'A SHORT HISTORY OF BOSTON' printed and published by The Guardian Press (Boston) Ltd., Nelson Way, Boston.

# HM BARK ENDEAVOUR

In 1786 Lieutenant James Cook, later to become the famous Captain Cook, set sail in HM Bark Endeavour. This was to be a voyage of exploration and scientific investigation which resulted in the discovery of what we now know as Australia and New Zealand. A replica of the Endeavour was launched in Australia in December 1993 and I first saw it in Sydney Harbour in January 1995. The replica circumnavigated the British Isles in 1997 making two visits to Boston. This entailed sailing up the River Witham to a tumultuous reception all the way to its moorings in Boston Dock. I had the privilege of being a guide on both occasions that I found most enjoyable and an exhilarating experience.

It was difficult, however, to visualise how ninety five men lived in such cramped conditions. The number was made up as follows: Lieut. J. Cook in Command of seventy-one crew. Twelve Marines were on board to maintain discipline, plus eleven civilians that included an Astronomer, Naturalist and two Artists. During the voyage from 1768 to 1771, twenty-nine died and one was discharged. Cook was the first Captain to substantially reduce the incidence of scurvy amongst his crew and to calculate his longitudinal position with accuracy.

# THE MERIDIAN LINE

The Greenwich Meridian Line passes through the reclaimed part of Kirton Marsh and therefore warrants a mention. This imaginary line that identifies longitude zero, is marked by a green line on Explorer Ordnance Survey maps that cover the areas involved. This invisible line crosses into England at Withernsea, East Yorkshire, crossing the Humber at Cleethorpes, down through Louth and Boston in Lincolnshire. It crosses the Wash just east of Fosdyke and on to the Royal Observatory in Greenwich, through Lewes and out over the channel at Peacehaven on the south coast in Sussex.

The Frampton Parish Council erected a stone where the Meridian Line crosses the road that leads from the Church down to the Marsh. Then to mark the year 2000 they erected a beacon on the opposite side of the road.

Where the line crosses the Kirton Marsh Road, a mixture of six oaks and lime trees have been planted to mark the year 2000. Three more have been planted where the line passes close to the site of the 'Black Houses'.

It was at the Washington Conference of 1884 that twenty-five countries met and eventually decided that the Zero Meridian should pass through the Observatory at Greenwich.

A Meridian is half of any of the imaginary great circles on the Earth's surface passing through both geographical poles and is used to indicate longitude which can be expressed in degrees, hours, minutes and seconds. Navigators can tell where they are in the sky or on the sea if they can calculate longitude and latitude.

Up until the late 18th Century navigators had not been able to measure their true position at sea, as there had been no instrumentation to accurately measure longitude. In 1716 an Act was passed by Parliament to reward the first person who could find longitude and a Board of Longitude was set up to adjudicate on solutions.

The reward eventually went to John Harrison who lived and worked in Barrow-on-Humber in North Lincolnshire. This is a story worth pursuing and books are available in libraries both on John Harrison's amazing achievement and the history of the Meridian Line.

# MAPS

Incidentally, I have two German Ordnance Survey maps that came into my possession in France in 1944, that outlines in detail the Wash and all inland areas of Lincolnshire. There was in fact a hanger half full of maps that covered the whole of the British Isles.

There was no need therefore, to take down signposts and obliterate names on farm and trade vehicles during World War II. With these maps the Germans, had they been allowed to enter the British Isles, could have almost found their way around the countryside blindfolded! See extracts of the maps on the next two pages.

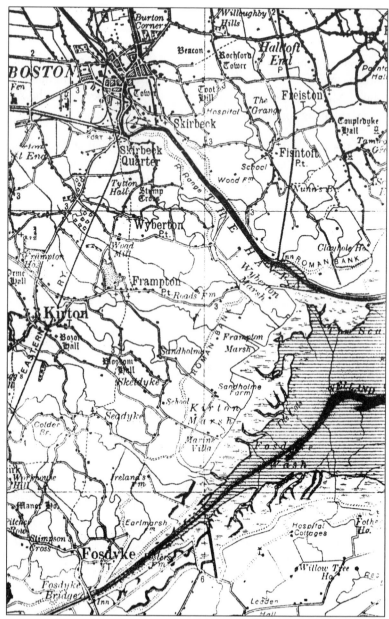

This is part of one of two German maps of Lincolnshire
I acquired when in France in 1944.

*Stanley Naylor, 2000*

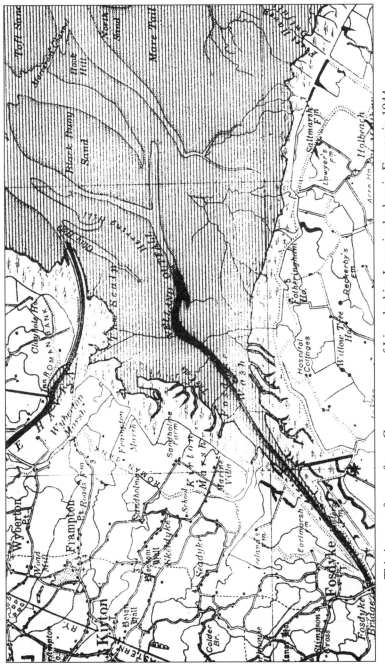

This is part of one of two German maps of Lincolnshire I acquired when in France in 1944.

*Stanley Naylor, 2000*

# SUMMARY OF KIRTON SKELDYKE
# AND THE MARSH IN THE YEAR 2000

Spring, Summer, Autumn and Winter. Seasons still come and go. Potatoes, corn and sugar beet are grown in the fields every year, exactly as it all happened over seventy years ago.

However, there are a few changes. Houses have been demolished and new ones built. The population in the district has declined owing to mechanisation taking over on the farms.

The skilled worker on the farms in the 1920's and 30's had to make a potato grave (clamp) and cover it to keep out hard frosts. Erecting a corn stack that would not fall over and thatching it to keep out the elements. Sinking rows of drainage pipes across fields by hand making sure the water would flow to the respective dykes. No, I don't have all these skills, but there were many fine men who did, and working with horses was a skill in its own right. Perhaps those types of skills are not required today, as the emphasis is on the workers being mechanically skilled.

The school building has recently been demolished and the church, chapel and pub are residential. The closing of the pub must have been a bitter blow (no pun intended), because in my mind the 'Boat & Gun' was the hub of activity in the close knit community.

The inhabitants of Skeldyke today enjoy all the 'mod cons' with everything operated by electricity, candles and paraffin lamps being obsolete but still handy when there is a power cut! En-suite facilities are in all the houses, telephones and televisions are part of every day life, and no doubt computers are appearing in some of them.

'Wheels' are used every day, that is the four wheel car type, not the two wheel cycle type we had to endure.

Now that Skeldyke enjoys all the modern facilities, and they have every right to do so, I wonder if the friendly neighbourly spirit still exists. The friendly neighbourly atmosphere was something we enjoyed so much in those years before World War II when the tranquil countryside was a healthy place to live, and peace reigned overall!

Kirton Marsh, of course, does not have the attraction that we enjoyed in our youth, now that far away places take only a short flight. The tide, however, still flows freely in and out of the Wash twice every twenty-four hours, just as it's been doing for centuries. Flood tides are as fascinating to observe today as they were in my youth *(see photo)*. A few Marsh flowers still adorn this vast area of muddy creeks and samphire is just as tasty whether cooked as a vegetable or pickled. I don't know of anyone today who is brave enough to swim in the 'Big Creek', so perhaps it's the wild-fowlers who get the most enjoyment from these estuarine flats.

Finally, it is alleged that just before he died, King John lost his jewels whilst crossing the Wash. The question is where? I have been looking for the past sixty odd years and found nothing!

*Stanley Naylor*

# LINCOLNSHIRE MUSEUMS

The Museums of Lincolnshire are highly recommended both for adults and a learning process in history for children. They each have a number of the same exhibits, but each one has unique exhibits not seen in the others. For example, Spalding has a punt boat, Lincoln has steam engines, Skegness has the shell of a 'mud and stud' house, Great Steeping have horses and Mauthorpe has a rare collection of horse brasses. Between them they have everything we used in the household and on the farm in the 1920's and 30's, either practical or shown in pictures.

## MUSEUM OF LINCOLNSHIRE LIFE
Burton Road, Lincoln. LN1 3LY
Tel: 01522 528448 - Fax: 01522 521264
Open every day May - September 10.00 am to 5.30 pm
Winter openings may differ

Lincolnshire's largest Social History Museum. This listed building built in 1857 houses a captivating arrangement of displays depicting the many aspects of Lincolnshire life. Tractors, farm implements, First World War tank, shops, post office, blacksmiths shop, a domestic gallery showing a nursery bedroom, kitchen, parlour and wash house. Note the huge turntable under the body of the steam engines from which a steel hawser pulled a four furrowed plough from the far end of a field. There is also a living van that would accompany a steam cultivating set, and much, much more!

## CHURCH FARM MUSEUM
Church Road South, Skegness. PE25 2HF
Tel/Fax: 01754 766658
Open every day April - October 10.30 am to 5.30 pm
Closed in the winter

The Museum has a fully furnished house in the 1920's/30's style, that I have tried to describe in the book. See the copper, dolly tub and peg, wringer, iron bedstead, black lead fire grate, long tin bath tub, water purifier, meat safe, bacon flitches and ham hung from the ceiling. Everything as it was between the two Wars. Blacksmith shop, farm implements and machinery are fully displayed.

The white thatched 'mud and stud' cottage is unique dating back to the eighteenth century and was opened in 1982 after being moved from Withern. This is a similar house to 'The Nook' in Kirton Skeldyke.

'BOB' is a unique Single Cylinder Steam Traction Engine 8 NHP with a firebox for burning inferior fuels. The engine was shipped to Tasmania in February 1892 and returned to the U.K. in 1988 in a sorry state. Major restoration work was undertaken by a local firm and now 'BOB' has pride of place at the Museum and I understand can be seen under steam on certain days of the year. Another interesting item is the two-way four furrowed plough that was pulled by steam engines.

Both Lincoln and Skegness Museums are in the care of Lincolnshire County Councils.

## NORTHCOTE HEAVY HORSE CENTRE
Great Steeping, Near Spilsby, Lincolnshire. PE20 5PS
Tel: 01754 830286

Here in the heart of one of the most attractive shire counties in rural England are horses that are the successors of those hard working horses that were on the farms in the 1930's. Take a journey back in time when horsepower was the only means of transporting goods and people. This is a great visit for children, they can help to brush and clean these lovely horses that are accustomed to being surrounded by people. The Carriage Museum displays many horse drawn vehicles.

## ASCOUGHFEE HALL MUSEUM AND GARDENS
Churchgate, Spalding, Lincolnshire. PE11 2RA
Tel: 01775 725468

Sitting beside the River Welland is this medieval hall built in the fifteenth century, the eight galleries of history are well worth exploring. The farming exhibits and pictures relating to the story of 'LINCOLNSHIRE COUNTRY LIFE' almost brings the era of the 1920's and 30's to life! One of the main exhibits relating to this book, is a punt (boat) and a muzzle loaded gun similar to the ones used by the Halls on Kirton Marsh.

Ascoughfee Hall was once the home of Maurice Johnson - a lawyer and antiquarian - who founded the 'Spalding Gentlemen's Society' in 1710.

The Museum is highly recommended and the landscape gardens are a picture! The Hall is also the Tourist Information Centre. Free admission, open all year round except for the winter weekends.

## MAUTHORPE MUSEUM
Located on the B1196 between Alford and Willoughby, Lincolnshire.
Tel: 01507 462336

This is a family run business, times of opening are restricted and there is a small admission fee.

It is well worth a visit to see some unique exhibits including a rare fairground organ. The household and social bygones are too numerous to mention in detail, there are also tools of rural trades and crafts, a 1926 farm wagon that has only a half-lock. There are tractors galore, a rare clover threshing drum and some seven hundred horse brasses, that is one of the finest collections I have ever seen.